MULTIENGINE
Airplane Rating

5TH REVISED EDITION

MULTIENGINE
AIRPLANE RATING

a guide to the FAA oral and flight tests

by T. M. Smith

A Zweng Manual, from

PAN AMERICAN NAVIGATION SERVICE

12021 VENTURA BLVD.
NORTH HOLLYWOOD, CALIF. 91604

MULTIENGINE AIRPLANE RATING

5th revised edition, 1975

First published in 1964, and previously revised in
1965, 1971, and 1973. Reprinted in 1967, 1968, and
1969. Copyright ©1964 by Pan American
Navigation Service, Inc., 12021 Ventura Blvd.,
North Hollywood, Calif. 91604. All rights reserved.
No part of this book may be reproduced in any
form or by any means without the written consent
of the publisher.

Printed in the U.S.A.

LC Catalog Card Number: 64-7947

ISBN: 0-87219-003-X

Preface

ONE OF THE most significant facts attendant upon the growth of the general aviation fleet in recent years is the striking increase in the number of corporate and privately owned multiengine airplanes. Currently there are almost 20,000 such aircraft flying in the U.S.—most of them in the class commonly referred to as light twins—with an FAA forecast of a 32,000 total by 1981. Meanwhile, the number of Multiengine Ratings issued to pilots has outpaced even the increase in the number of active multiengine airplanes.

The reasons for this accelerating interest in multiengine airplanes are not hard to find. The most obvious one is the dollars-and-cents efficiency with which the light twin serves businesses, both large and small, as a go-anywhere-anytime transport. A less obvious but almost equally compelling reason is the higher utility of the light twin as compared to the single-engine plane. To the private owner, utility means more night flying, more instrument flying, and longer trips, including the transcontinental and even transoceanic.

Today's aircraft engines are refined to a high degree of reliability and an in-flight failure is rare, but pilots who fly night and IFR inevitably begin to think in terms of the additional safety a twin provides. That pilots are qualifying themselves to fly the twins is borne out by the surging interest in the Multiengine Rating. Probably even more would acquire the Rating if they didn't stand a little in awe of the twin, looking upon it as an intimidatingly complex machine beyond the capabilities of the average single-engine pilot

It is the purpose of this book to dispel such notions, to help the pilot acquire his Multiengine Rating with knowledge and ease, and to serve as a reference text for his future use.

No written examination of any kind is required for the Multiengine Rating—only oral questioning by the FAA examiner (see Chapter 11) and the actual flight test on multiengine procedures.

T. M. Smith

Contents

MULTIENGINE
Airplane Rating

Pressurized Cessna 340. (*Cessna Aircraft Corp.*)

1.

Multiengine procedures and techniques

The first step toward a Multiengine Rating should be the reading of the Pilot's Operating Manual, or Owner's Handbook, for the airplane to be used. After having read the manual, take it with you to the airplane. Sit in the cockpit studying the control systems, switches, selectors, instruments, fuel valves, and trim tabs until you can locate them without looking and until you understand their operation.

A twin-engine airplane may look complicated at first, but it will help if you realize that much of the additional gadgetry is simply duplication of engine controls and instruments, and that there are no new controls with functions different from those to be found in a high-performance single-engine airplane. Thus you will find *two* throttles, *two* propeller controls, *two* mixture controls, *two* gas valves, *two* tachometers, *two* manifold pressure gauges, and *two* sets of engine temperature and pressure gauges, all of which, taken singly, you would understand if you are acquainted with them from having flown single-engine airplanes such as the Beech Bonanza, Cessna Skylane, Piper Comanche, Mooney, Meyers, Navion, Bellanca, or similar

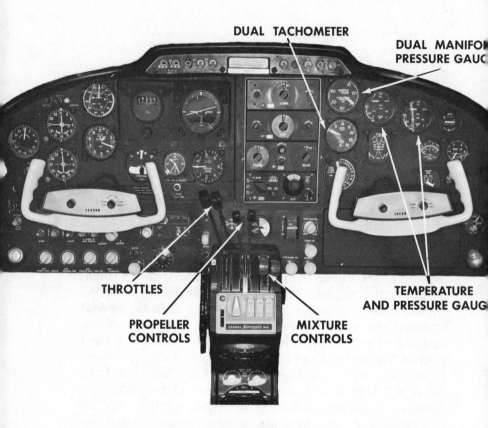

Instrument panel of a modern light twin. Note duplication of throttle, propeller, and mixture controls on pedestal in center; dual tachometer, manifold pressure, temperature, and pressure gauges on right. (*Cessna Aircraft Co.*)

aircraft. Even having flown only single-engine aircraft without propeller controls, you would find most other items to be familiar.

You should begin your twin-engine flight training with the understanding that procedures and checklists will be even more important than in single-engine aircraft, and that these habits should be formed as soon as possible.

The following paragraphs explain the procedures and techniques you should be familiar with in multiengine operation.

PREFLIGHT

The Owner's Manual specifies the items to be checked and sequences to be followed in conducting a pre-flight inspection. These steps should be adhered to systematically. A typical pre-flight checklist is shown in Fig. 1.

These procedures vary with the aircraft, but in general the practice is to start at one definite point on the airplane, usually the ignition switches and internal control locks. From there, work completely around the airplane until back at the starting point. The check should be thorough, and you should understand the purpose of each item checked.

STARTING

The Pilot's Flight Handbook should be followed for the starting operation. Only some general considerations can be given here.

The landing gear switch or selector should always be checked for *down* positioning before turning on the master electrical switch if the gear works electrically, and before starting engines if the gear operates hydraulically. It is possible for the gear switch or selector to have been kicked or placed in the *up* position accidentally. If it goes un-

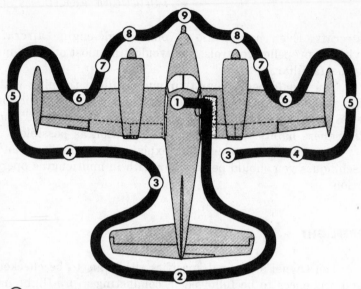

(1)
a. Remove controls lock.
b. Momentarily turn on battery switch, and check fuel quantity gages.

(2)
a. Remove external surface locks, if installed.
b. Check general condition of elevator, rudder and trim tab hinges, hinge bolts and actuator rod bolts.
c. Remove tie-down.

(3)
a. Check static pressure source hole for obstruction.
b. Open baggage door (right side only) and check oxygen pressure gage and make sure sufficient oxygen remains for intended flight. Check that oxygen face masks and hoses are available.
c. Close baggage door and check for security.

(4)
a. Check aileron and tab hinges, and hinge and actuator rod bolts.

(5)
a. Check main fuel tank filler cap and fairing cover for security.

(6)
a. Check auxiliary tank filler cap and cover for security.
b. Check battery compartment cover panel for security (left side only).
c. If ice is anticipated, check fluid level in anti-ice reservoir. Check anti-ice reservoir compartment cover panel for security (right side only).
d. Check auxiliary tank vent for obstruction.
e. Check landing light for damage.
f. Remove wing tie-down.

(7)
a. Check oil level. Minimum 9 quarts; fill to 12 quarts for extended flight.
b. Check main landing gear strut and tire inflation. Check gear door for security.
c. On first flight of the day, drain two ounces of fuel from the strainer. If water is detected in fuel, drain fuel tank sumps.

(8)
a. Check propeller and spinner for nicks, cracks and security.
b. Check oil filler cap for security through cooling air inlet in cowl nose cap.
c. Check cowl access doors for security.

(9)
a. Check nose gear strut and tire inflation, nose gear doors for security.
b. Check pitot tube opening for obstructions.
c. Check taxi light for damage.
d. Remove tie-down.

Repeat steps "4" through "8."

Fig. 1—A typical pre-flight inspection. *(Cessna Aircraft Co.)*

noticed, turning on the master electrical switch could cause an electrically operated gear to retract, and starting an engine equipped with a hydraulic pump might cause the same result to hydraulically operated gears.

After starting, check the oil pressure gauges. If no indication appears after 30 seconds, the engine should be shut down and the trouble investigated.

If the engine fails to start, two common causes are insufficient priming and over-priming, with the latter more prevalent in warm weather or with a hot engine. In this case it will usually be effective to start the engine with throttle wide open, mixture set to idle cut-off, and ignition switches *on*, quickly reversing positions of throttle and mixture controls when the engine fires. The Owner's Manual should be consulted for recommendations.

TAXIING

There are some general considerations applicable to taxiing both tailwheel and tricycle gear twin-engine airplanes. The visibility over the nose is sufficient in either type to make taxiing S-turns unnecessary. The engines are used for directional control. To make the airplane turn right, left throttle is advanced slightly, and the unbalanced thrust turns the airplane to the right. (Fig. 2.)

Brakes should be used sparingly for controlling the speed of the airplane. They may be used conservatively in starting and stopping turns. While inside brake may be applied to shorten the turning radius in taxiing and parking, care should be taken to keep the inside wheel rolling slightly. This prevents wear on the tire. Brakes should not be "ridden" constantly for directional control since this will cause unnecessary wear, possible overheating, and possible subsequent failure.

The pilot taxiing a multiengine airplane should be cognizant of its probable greater wing span and length, looking out and around carefully so that he will not taxi

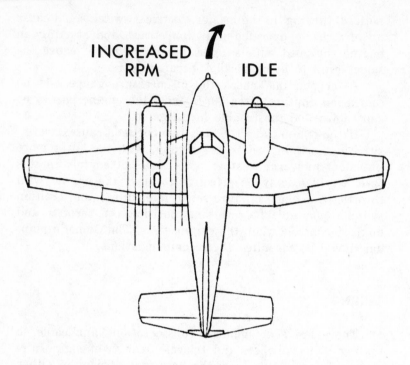

Fig. 2—Advancing the left throttle causes the airplane to turn to the right in taxiing.

the wing tips into or swing the tail against anything.

The increased propwash of a twin-engine airplane will require vigilance from the pilot to assure that no damage from its blast occurs to smaller aircraft, bystanders, or hangar areas.

In tricycle gear twins, taxiing is easier due to the steerable nosewheel. On light twins the nosewheel is connected to the rudder pedals, left rudder turning the nosewheel to the left, and vice versa. Taxiing in a straight line, as well as gentle turns, can be accomplished by setting the engines at the same rpm and steering with the rudder. For shorter turns and more precise maneuvering, the outside throttle can be advanced and the inside throttle retarded to start the turn. Then the inside throttle should be brought back up and the outside throttle closed to straighten out the turn.

In taxiing a conventional twin-engine airplane with a tailwheel, the rudder will not be effective; directional control must be maintained by using the throttles and occasionally "snubbing" the brake lightly. The throttle tension or friction lock should be loose enough while taxiing to allow free and easy movement of the throttles.

When one throttle is advanced for directional control, the other throttle must be closed completely at the same time, so that the advanced throttle will not have to be opened as much. Failure to do so leads to excessive speed, overcontrolling, and violent braking correction.

Conventional gear twins usually have a tailwheel lock, which is normally unlocked for taxiing and locked for takeoffs and landings. However, the tailwheel lock may be locked for taxiing in a straight line, particularly in a cross-wind where it will help counteract the tendency of the airplane to weathercock into the wind. In cross-wind taxiing, the throttle setting of the upwind engine should be increased to prevent weathercocking.

When the tailwheel has been locked, the pilot should remember to unlock it before attempting a turn, or abnormal side loads may be developed in the tail section.

In both conventional and tricycle gear twin-engine aircraft, the pilot should devote one hundred per cent attention to his taxiing, with particular care in avoiding high speed and complacency.

CHECKLIST

The pilot must understand the absolute necessity of using a checklist prior to takeoffs and landings. Multiengine airplanes have more items to check than single-engine types, and mis-positioning or improper settings lead to more serious consequences than in the single-engine types.

For example, improperly set trim tabs could cause a condition the pilot might not be able to overpower. If he were to attempt a takeoff with the trim tabs still set tail-heavy after a landing, the resultant nose-up attitude on takeoff might create control forces the pilot was not strong enough to overcome until he had re-set the trim. It is much easier and safer to have the tabs set correctly at the beginning, and they will be set correctly if the checklist is used properly.

Most modern airplanes are equipped with checklists supplied by the manufacturer, and these should be followed, with any revisions made necessary by variation of the equipment of individual airplanes.

Where there are two pilots, one pilot should read the checklist and the other should perform the operations indicated. The pilot performing the check should touch each control and point to each item checked.

A typical checklist would cover these items, not necessarily in the order given, for a *Before Takeoff* check:

1. Landing gear switches or controls in *down* position.
2. Elevator and rudder trim tabs set for takeoff.
3. Throttle friction tightened.
4. Mixtures rich.
5. Propeller controls forward.
6. Flaps up, or as desired.
7. Fuel selectors on main tanks.
8. Fuel quantity checked.
9. Carburetor heat controls cold.
10. Oil shutters as necessary to control oil temp.
11. Engine instruments in *green* range.
12. Altimeter set.
13. Gyros uncaged and set.
14. Booster pumps on.
15. Controls free and movement in proper direction.
16. Cowl flaps open.
17. Doors and windows locked.
18. Run-up; check mags, prop controls, carburetor heat,

and generator output.

A typical *Before Landing* checklist will be shown in the paragraphs on "Approaches and Landings."

TAKEOFF

After completing the *Before Takeoff* check, the pilot should taxi to the center of the runway and line up with it. If the aircraft has a tailwheel lock, it should be locked after the airplane has rolled ahead for a few feet in a straight line. In the conventional or tailwheel aircraft, the rudder control will not be effective at first, and the pilot must maintain directional control by differential, opening of the throttles to takeoff power. The pilot can anticipate torque effects and lead with the left throttle slightly in this type of airplane. As the airplane begins to gather speed the control wheel should be eased forward to bring the nose to flying position and neutralized to keep it there. Brakes should be used for directional control only if throttles and rudder are ineffective. During takeoff the pilot's heels should rest on the floor with the toes on the bottom of the pedals unless braking becomes necessary. If a serious swing develops during takeoff the pilot should cut both throttles and stop the airplane as soon as possible.

On aircraft with unsupercharged engines the throttles are opened fully during takeoff, but with supercharged engines the pilot must watch the manifold pressure gauges during takeoff, stopping the throttles at the maximum recommended by the manufacturer.

Takeoffs are easier in a tricycle gear airplane since the steerable nosewheel is effective throughout the takeoff run, and differential use of the throttles is not usually necessary.

Engine-out considerations. Before beginning a takeoff, three important speeds should be fixed firmly in the pilot's mind: (1) minimum control speed, (2) single-engine best-rate-of-climb speed, and (3) single-engine best-angle-of-climb speed. These speeds are defined as follows:

Minimum control speed—The airspeed below which the airplane cannot be controlled in flight with one engine operating at takeoff power and the other engine windmilling. This speed is known as Vmc.

Single-engine best-rate-of-climb speed — The airspeed which delivers the greatest gain in altitude in the shortest time with gear up, flaps up, dead engine feathered.

Single-engine best-angle-of-climb speed — The airspeed which delivers the greatest gain in altitude in the shortest horizontal distance with gear up, flaps up, and dead engine feathered.

The airplane should be held on the ground during takeoff until it reaches the minimum control speed. It should then be lifted off and accelerated as rapidly as possible to the single-engine best-rate-of-climb speed if no obstacles are ahead, or to the single-engine best-angle-of-climb speed until the obstacles are cleared and then V_y (twin-engine maximum rate of climb airspeed) should be maintained for a few hundred feet; this will provide the most altitude in the shortest time, thus placing the aircraft in the most favorable situation possible should an engine fail. Altitude above the ground is far more desirable than excess airspeed above V_y.

AFTER TAKEOFF

The gear should be retracted when it is evident that the airplane can not land back on the runway should an emergency develop, i.e., the gear should not be pulled up with a long runway in front of the pilot which could still be landed on should an engine quit.

When the gear is retracted the brakes should be depressed so that the wheels will be stopped when they enter the wheel wells. This will add to the life of the tires since rubber will not be burned off by the spinning wheel fitting snugly into its well.

After gear retraction the power should be reduced to the *climb* power settings recommended by the manufacturer. On most aircraft, manifold pressure is reduced first, then rpm, but there are some exceptions, notably on the Aero Commanders and Beech Twin Bonanzas powered by the unsupercharged Lycoming GO-480 Series, where rpm only is reduced and throttles left wide open, allowing an enrichening jet to produce additional cooling. Manufacturers' recommendations should be strictly observed, however, as in other aircraft, reducing rpm before manifold pressure can lead to detonation, overheating, and excessive load on the engine with possible engine damage.

To maintain a constant manifold pressure during climb, the throttles will have to be advanced about one inch per thousand feet since this is the rate at which atmospheric pressure decreases.

CRUISING

Upon reaching cruising altitude, power charts of the manufacturer should be consulted for the desired performance. For most purposes 65% power represents a good balance between speed and economy. Settings above and below this can be used for special needs. In reducing to cruising power settings, manifold pressure should be reduced first, then rpm. The manifold pressure should be brought back to 1″ to 2″ below the desired setting, and when the rpm is decreased the manifold pressure will climb 1″ to 2″. Observation of the individual aircraft characteristics will tell the pilot how much increase of manifold pressure will be encountered.

Straight and level flight in twin-engine airplanes presents no special problems, as multiengine aircraft are somewhat more stable than single-engine types. Occasionally, in the first few flights, minor difficulty is encountered in determining the proper nose position, but this can be overcome by referring to the sensitive altimeter. When the trend of the altimeter has stopped, the nose is in the proper cruise position for the power being used.

It will be necessary to keep the engines synchronized, and this must be done by ear since the tachometers are not quite exact enough for the purpose. If the engines are not synchronized you will hear an uneven beat, a sound something like "Unh, unh, unh . . ." The faster this beat is, the farther apart the engines are. Set the propeller controls at the same rpm and then listen for the beat. If the beat *is* heard, only one propeller control should be moved; if the beat gets slower, the prop control is being moved in the proper direction. Finally, as you move the prop control ever more slightly and wait for a change, the beat will disappear altogether.

In trimming the multiengine airplane you will find the trim tabs even more important than in a single due to the greater weight, speed ranges, power, and possible loading configurations.

Re-trim the aircraft for each change of attitude, power, or speed; otherwise you will be trying to overpower the controls. This constant fighting the controls can wear you out unduly and detract from the airplane's performance. The proper method of trimming the airplane is to place it in the desired attitude with the controls, then use the trim to relieve the control pressure.

STALLS

The pilot should practice stalls and recoveries for the same reasons as in single-engine aircraft—to acquaint himself with the characteristics of the airplane as it approaches a stall, the stalls themselves, and the recoveries. The pilot should observe the warning the aircraft gives as it approaches the stall, note the airspeeds in various configurations, and observe the aircraft's response to stall recovery. Since more altitude may be lost than in a single-engine aircraft, stalls should not be practiced below 3,000 feet.

A conventional-geared twin rolling out after landing. *(Beech Aircraft Corp.)*

They *should* be practiced, however, in turn, with gear and flaps down.

APPROACH AND LANDING

The power and speed should be reduced on the downwind leg until the airplane is down to landing-gear-extension speed. If a manufacturers checklist is not available, the mnemonic *GUMP* is an excellent pre-landing check. The *G* stands for gas, which would mean fuel valves to main tanks, quantity checked, and booster pumps on. The *U* is for undercarriage, meaning gear down, indicators checked down, gear checked down visually if possible, and landing gear warning horn checked. *M* represents mixture, for mixture rich, and *P* is for propellers, with those controls advanced as applicable.

Flaps may be lowered progressively as necessary. Many models recommend the use of a small amount of flap (15°) immediately following gear extension. Thereafter, flaps can be lowered as necessary.

Power is used on the approaches in multiengine airplanes since these airplanes have steep rates of descent with power off. This is owing to their greater weight and wing loading, as well as the fact that the flaps are usually quite effective in producing a steep gliding angle. This angle can be controlled with power, the airspeed being controlled with the elevators and the descent with the throttles.

The actual touchdown can be accomplished with or without power. One method is to carry power until the flareout, and then cut it, holding the aircraft off until touchdown without power. However, many pilots prefer never to cut the throttles completely until touchdown.

During the descent, power changes should be smooth and steady, and the final approach airspeed held constant with the elevators. The airspeed on final should not be less than the minimum control speed on one engine; if maximum power were to be applied in an emergency, the loss of one engine would mean loss of control.

The manufacturer's recommendations will give the pilot an approach airspeed to use, and this speed should provide the pilot with sufficient control to flare out, with a minimum amount of floating during the "holding off" stage. Too much speed will make for excessive floating and possible ballooning, whereas too *little* speed will cause the airplane to drop onto the ground while the pilot is trying to flare it out.

On most tail-wheel type airplanes the general practice is to make wheel landings, lowering the tail slowly after touchdown. This applies to such airplanes as the Beech 18 series, DC-3, Lodestar, and Cessna T-50 or UC-78.

Tricycle gear airplanes should be landed slightly tail low so that the two main wheels touch before the nose wheel; damage to the nose wheel can result from its contacting the ground heavily.

On tail-wheel airplanes, directional control is maintained with rudder during the roll out. The amount of control diminishes with the speed; be ready with throttles and brakes during the latter stages of the landing roll. For example, if you are landing with a right cross-wind be alert for the airplane to swerve to the right. Counteract this swerve with left rudder, left brake, and right engine.

At the end of the landing run before turning off the runway, the tail wheel should be unlocked. If a side load is put on the tail wheel before unlocking, it could cause abnormal structural loads in the tail section. In addition, you probably won't be able to unlock the tail wheel until you have shifted the load in the opposite direction with brakes.

CROSS-WIND TAKEOFF AND LANDING

Observe the limitations of the airplane in a cross-wind. Most airplanes aren't designed to operate in a 90° cross-wind of more than .2 of the stalling speed. Some airplane handbooks incorporate a Maximum Safe Cross-Wind Graph in their instructions (See Fig. 3).

During a cross-wind takeoff, up-wind aileron should be used to help hold the up-wind wing down, and it will be helpful to apply power on the up-wind engine a little in advance of the other engine, particularly on a tail-wheel airplane because the rudders on these airplanes are ineffective at slow speeds. On a tail-wheel airplane the tail should be held down a little longer than usual, since the locked tail wheel will prevent weathervaning into the wind. After the rudder has become effective the tail should be raised and then takeoff power applied to both engines equally. Make sure the airplane has sufficient flying speed before pulling the airplane off the runway; if it settles back to the ground, drifting, the landing gear can be damaged.

Crosswind landings in multiengine airplanes differ little from those in single-engine airplanes. Drift can be counteracted by either crabbing or holding the up-wind

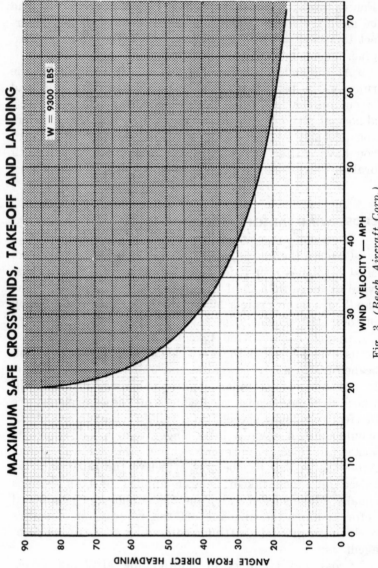

Fig. 3. *(Beech Aircraft Corp.)*

wing down. Our recommendation is a combination of the best features of both, in which the crabbing method (heading the airplane into the wind) is used during the early part of the approach to keep the airplane's path lined up with the runway, and then as the airplane crosses the boundary of the airport the nose is swung gently with the rudder to line up with the runway, the up-wind wing being lowered simultaneously. Opposite rudder is maintained as necessary to keep the airplane from turning in the direction of the lowered wing, and touchdown is made on the up-wind wheel first.

On a tail-wheel airplane, after touchdown you should be especially alert to keep the airplane from weathercocking into the wind, particularly as the tail is lowered and the rudder loses its effectiveness. The weathervaning or swerving can be counteracted with down-wind rudder and brake and up-wind engine.

GO-AROUND PROCEDURE

If it becomes necessary to decide whether or not to go around again in an approach, make the decision while you've still got as much altitude as possible under the circumstances—the more altitude and speed you have, the easier it will be. The steps:

(1) Apply takeoff power.
(2) Retract flaps to takeoff position if specified; otherwise, retract flaps completely.
(3) As flaps retract, increase pitch attitude to prevent sinking. Maintain V_x until obstacles are cleared, then maintain V_y.
(4) Retract landing gear *after positive climb indicated.*
(5) Re-trim.
(6) Climb out at V_y.

Consult the operator's handbook for specific recommendations; the procedures will vary slightly with different airplanes, and the airspeeds to use will be spelled out for each.

Some general considerations are:

Takeoff power should be applied smoothly. On some aircraft the sudden ramming open of the throttles could cause a flooding of the carburetor with resultant engine failure as well as possible internal damage to the engine.

Be prepared to apply forward elevator pressure until you can get the airplane re-trimmed; normally you would have the airplane trimmed tail-heavy during the approach.

If at all possible, make the decision to go around while above VMC. Otherwise, you would not have directional control of the airplane if one engine should fail.

For many years the standard go-around procedure called for retracting gear before flaps. However, it is now considered preferable to bring flaps up first, rotating the pitch attitude to prevent settling, and bringing the gear up only after a positive climb is indicated. Then if the aircraft should settle to the ground it will be less damaging for the fully extended gear to contact the ground than to have the gear touch while in process of retracting, or, if retracted, for propellers, flaps, or wings to make ground contact.

Engine to spare: Piper Twin Comanche with right engine feathered.
(Piper Aircraft Corp.)

2.

Single-engine procedures

The twin-engine airplane has no safety advantage over the single-engine airplane until it has reached the engine-out minimum control speed, or VMC. During the takeoff run prior to reaching VMC be prepared to throttle back both engines immediately should an engine failure occur, bringing the airplane to a stop as soon as possible. Keep your hand on the throttle throughout the takeoff so that no time will be wasted if this sudden action becomes necessary.

After reaching VMC, the following procedure should be used:

(1) Hold the airplane straight with hard rudder pressure.

(2) Push *both* propeller controls forward.

(3) Push *both* throttle controls forward.

(4) Push *both* mixture controls forward.

(5) Check: gear up, flaps up.

(6) Throttle back *dead* engine (heavy foot: good engine; dead foot: dead engine).

(7) Feather *dead* engine.

(8) Reduce power on operating engine as appropriate

for single-engine climb or single engine cruise.

(9) Trim.

(10) Isolate dead engine: gas off, ignition off, mixture idle cut-off, generator off, booster pump off.

The reasons for these steps are as follows:

1. When an engine fails, the airplane will swerve toward the dead engine owing to the unequal thrust. This yaw must be counteracted with hard rudder pressure.

2. Both propeller controls should be pushed forward On a non-supercharged engine, the prop controls should go all the way forward to give maximum r.p.m. Manufacturer's recommendations should be followed for supercharged engines. *Both* propeller controls are advanced to insure that the correct one goes forward. Propeller controls are advanced prior to throttles to prevent damage to the cylinders resulting from high manifold pressure and low r.p.m.

3. Both throttles should be pushed forward immediately after the propeller controls. On a non-supercharged engine, the throttles should be pushed wide open. Manufacturer's recommendations should be followed on supercharged engine. *Both* throttles are advanced to insure that the proper one has been selected.

4. Both mixture controls should be advanced to full rich to prevent detonation due to a too lean mixture at high power settings. *Both* mixture controls are advanced to insure that the proper one has been selected.

5. Gear and flaps should be retracted since the extra drag can prevent the airplane from climbing or even maintaining altitude.

6. By throttling back the engine you intend to feather, you have double-checked the identification of the dead engine. When the throttle is retarded there should be no change in the sound, the trim, and the power developed. If any of these occur, the wrong throttle has been retarded. The throttle can then be re-opened without any irreparable damage having been done.

7. After the engine has been identified in step 6, the

It takes only one: Cessna 320 with left engine feathered. *(Cessna Aircraft Corp.)*

dead engine propeller control should carefully be moved to the feather position and the engine feathered. Feathering is of the utmost importance. First, you must not feather the wrong engine. Second, most light twins will neither climb nor maintain altitude until the drag of the windmilling propeller is eliminated.

8. Manifold pressure and r.p.m. should be reduced to the manufacturer's recommendations for single-engine climb or single-engine cruise, whichever you are attempting. This will vary with altitude, temperature, loading, and individual airplanes, and occasionally it may be necessary to maintain full power until a safe altitude is reached.

9. Now you should relieve the rudder pressure by trimming the airplane with the rudder trim. If an aileron trip is available it should be used to help hold the wing on the "good engine side" a degree or two low. It will be

necessary to adjust the elevator trim since the power reduction caused by the failure of one engine will have made the airplane nose heavy.

10. Securing the dead engine is the last step; this can be accomplished after those steps more vital to staying in the air have been completed. However, the shutting off of the gas, ignition, mixture, and generator should be performed meticulously inasmuch as the operation of the controls for the wrong engine could be disastrous unless corrected. For engines with smaller capacity generators the electrical load should be reduced as much as possible during a single-engine cruise.

Your choice of airspeeds will vary with the conditions encountered. Should an engine fail after VMC on take-off, maintain the single-engine best-*angle*-of-climb airspeed until over obstacles, and then maintain the single-engine best *rate* of climb airspeed until reaching a sufficient altitude to complete a traffic pattern.

If the engine fails during cruising flight at altitude, use the manufacturer's recommendations for power at single-engine cruise. These settings would be somewhat higher than normal cruise for both engines.

If the engine fails on takeoff and there is sufficient runway to land again, throttles should be closed and the airplane landed, even if the airplane has reached VMC. Of course, if it has *not* reached VMC you have no choice but to stop because the airplane will not be controllable in flight.

SINGLE-ENGINE APPROACH AND LANDING

Generally the pilot properly flies a somewhat higher pattern than normal. Pre-landing check should be performed on the base leg rather than downwind, and the landing gear lowered there. The rudder trim should be neutralized at this point so that it will not be an adverse factor during the latter stages of the landing when the power is reduced. The final approach should be high, and the flaps should not be lowered until the pilot is sure of making the field. The pilot must make every effort to avoid being too low at any time since the airplane won't climb with gear or flaps down.

The final approach, then, should be a fairly steep, powered approach. A rule of thumb would be to leave the flaps up until it appears as though the airplane would land in the last half of the runway, flaps being lowered to bring the airplane's glide path to the first half of the runway.

SINGLE-ENGINE GO-AROUND

Concentrate on making your single-engine landing on your first attempt because in some cases a go-around may be impossible. Make the decision to go-around as early in the approach as possible, preferably above 300-400 feet of altitude and before full flaps have been lowered. Full power should be applied, gear brought up, and flaps upped in stages. Some altitude will be lost during this process, and the go-around should not be attempted unless you have sufficient altitude to raise gear and flaps.

In some models of airplanes, under specific circumstances, a go-around may be impossible. For example, on an airplane with hydraulically operated gear and flaps, the hydraulic pump on left engine only, and the left engine feathered, it would be necessary to lower the gear and flaps by means of the hydraulic hand pump. It would also be necessary to raise gear flaps by hand pumping, and this could easily take more time and altitude than you have available in which to go around.

SINGLE-ENGINE PRACTICE

Single-engine operation on takeoff can be simulated at altitude. The airplane should be slowed to the minimum control speed, placed in the takeoff attitude, gear down, and both throttles opened to takeoff power. Engine failure can be simulated by moving one mixture control to idle cutoff; single-engine procedure, as previously explained, should be followed, with the mixture brought back to rich and throttle opened to 10-12 inches of mercury to simulate zero thrust. Note the altitude when the engine fails and observe your own and the airplane's ability to remain above this figure and effect a climb. In this way, a reasonably accurate appraisal can be made of the problems in an engine failure on takeoff, particularly at the altitude used.

Practice single-engine landings as often as feasible, simulating zero thrust by having one throttle set to 10-12 inches of manifold pressure. Don't begin to practice feathering an engine until you are thoroughly proficient in single-engine landings because it can be difficult sometimes to unfeather an engine, necessitating a single-engine landing.

When feathering is practiced it should be done above 3,000 feet and with an airport nearby.

FEATHERING CONTROLS

On light twins, the most widely used feathering system is located on the propeller control, and feathering is accomplished by pulling the propeller control all the way aft. However, some of the larger light twins have separate feathering buttons. Feathering is accomplished here by pushing the button down or in.

To unfeather an engine which incorporates feathering on the propeller control itself, the following procedure is recommended:

Gas ....*ON*
Ignition ....*ON*
Mixture ....*RICH*
Booster Pump ..*USE AS IN NORMAL GROUND START*

Prop Control ....*FORWARD*
Starter ....*ENGAGE*

When the engine starts, it should be allowed to warm up at approximately 15 inches of manifold pressure until the cylinder temperature is in the green.

To unfeather an engine with feathering button controls, the following procedure is recommended:

Gas ....*ON*
Ignition ....*ON*
Mixture ....*RICH*
Prop control ......*DECREASE RPM*
Booster pump ....*USE AS IN NORMAL GROUND START*
Feather button ..*PUSH AND HOLD UNTIL ENGINE IS RUNNING APPROXIMATELY 800-1,000 RPM, THEN RELEASE*

The throttle and propeller controls should then be set for reduced power until the cylinder temperature is in the green.

ACCUMULATORS

Some twin-engine airplanes carry as optional equipment an air-oil type accumulator unit to assist the unfeathering process. This installation is found on airplanes which use the propeller control to accomplish feathering. In its operation, oil pressure at approximately 300 psi is retained in the accumulator when the engine is feathered. When the propeller control is moved forward the oil under pressure in the accumulator flows through the high rpm passage of the governor out to the propeller piston, returning the blades to low pitch. This results in the engine's windmilling without use of the starter.

To unfeather an engine equipped with an accumulator, proceed as follows:

Gas ....ON
Ignition ....ON
Mixture ....RICH
Booster pump ....USE AS IN NORMAL GROUND START
Prop control ......FORWARD

The throttle and propeller controls should be set for reduced power until the cylinder temperature is in the green.

*   *   *

All multiengine pilots should be familiar with the informative contents of FAA Aviation Safety Release No. 400, which is concerned primarily with engine-out minimum control speed and engine-out best climb speed. The release is reprinted here in its entirety.

FLIGHT EMERGENCIES
IN LIGHT TWIN-ENGINE AIRCRAFT

Aviation Safety Release No. 400

The recent increase in the use of twin-engine airplanes in general aviation has emphasized the importance of a practical knowledge of emergency procedures. Twin-engine airplanes are now operated by many pilots who have little formal transition training and no apprenticeship as second pilot in multiengine airplanes.

Modern twin-engine airplanes deliver excellent flight performance, reliability, and safety if handled properly by pilots who know how to use them. This release is intended to point out certain features of the flight characteristics of twin-engine airplanes which require pilot techniques beyond those required by single-engine airplanes.

For safety in twin-engine airplanes, familiarity with two speeds is vital: (1) *engine-out minimum control speed*—the airspeed below which the airplane cannot be controlled in flight with one engine operating at full power; and (2) *engine-out best climb speed*—the airspeed which delivers the best rate of climb or slowest descent with one engine out. This may be very close to the engine-out minimum control speed.

Three important principles to remember in twin-engine airplanes are:

1. *Altitude is more valuable to safety after takeoff than airspeed in excess of the best rate of climb speed.* In the event of an engine failure, excess airspeed is lost much more rapidly than altitude.

2. *Climb or continued level flight is impossible with gear extended and a propeller windmilling* in many current twin-engined airplanes. The airplane must be cleaned up immediately if flight is to continue.

3. *After an engine failure at cruising, meto power should be applied immediately.* The operating engine should be throttled back only when and if level flight is definitely established.

The engine-out minimum control speed is available from the manufacturer's airplane flight manual and may be confirmed by experiment. The speed published is established for the most critical condition—the airplane fully loaded and full takeoff power on the operating engine. Since the power output increases at lower altitudes, engine-out control loss is more critical on takeoff, especially from airports at low elevations.

A multiengine pilot must know and observe this minimum control speed. Any attempt to continue flight on one engine at a lower speed will result in a loss of control and a probable crash.

In the event of a sudden engine failure at an airspeed below the engine-out minimum control speed, the operating engine must be throttled immediately to a point at which flight control can be maintained. If this power will not prevent a loss of altitude, an immediate landing must be effected. Banking slightly (not more than 5°) toward the operating engine will aid in maintaining flight control without appreciable loss of lift effectiveness.

In many current twin-engined airplanes, unlike some of the older multiengined airplanes, the engine-out minimum control speed may be as much as 20 mph above the normal stalling speed of the airplane.

The engine-out best climb speed is found in the airplane flight manual. It is the airspeed which gives the best rate of climb. The airspeed which gives the steepest angle of climb (for clearing obstacles) is usually slower and may be also found in the flight manual.

Great care must be observed in maintaining either of these speeds for two reasons: (1) they require prolonged flight at speeds very close to the engine-out minimum control speed; and (2) a deviation of only a few mph from the prescribed speeds results in a significant decrease in climb performance. A loss of climb will result just as certainly from an airspeed which is too high as from one which is too low.

When a pilot assumes the responsibility for a twin-engine airplane, he should determine from a reliable source, or by experiment, in what *configurations of gear, flaps, and propeller the airplane will maintain altitude* with a full load and engine out. Experiments should be made at full gross weight, using the best rate of climb speed for at least five minutes. Several fatal accidents have resulted from attempts to pull up for a go-around with gear down when the airplane was actually incapable of climbing in this configuration.

To establish single-engine flight after an engine failure in cruising flight, *it is recognized practice to apply maximum allowable power* to the operating engine until level flight is clearly established. If the airplane is found to be capable of level flight or climb with the existing load, altitude, and temperature, appropriate power reduction can be made. In no case should the airspeed be allowed to fall below the engine-out best climb speed, even though altitude is lost, since this speed will always provide the best chance of climb or the least altitude loss.

The ability to climb at approximately 50 feet per minute in calm air is necessary to maintain level flight for protracted periods in even moderate turbulence.

A pilot with predominantly single-engine training and experience who proposes to fly a twin-engine airplane should study thoroughly all available technical information on its performance and the operation of its accessories and emergency equipment. He should arrange for a substantial amout of transition instruction from a competent instructor, and should learn and practice all normal and emergency operations appropriate to the airplane involved.

He should familiarize himself with the following general procedures for use in the event of a sudden engine failure:

1. **Failure during takeoff or climb-out.**

   (a) *If airspeed is below engine-out minimum control speed*—reduce power to maintain flight control, and gain speed if possible. Since you should never climb higher than necessary to clear immediate obstructions before engine-out best climb speed is attained, an immediate landing is usually imperative.

   (b) *If airspeed is below engine-out best climb speed*—attain that speed before attempting to climb.

   (c) *If airspeed is at or above engine-out best climb speed*—keep maximum available power on good engine and hold engine-out best climb speed. If climb results, maneuver carefully for landing back at airport, otherwise prepare for landing at nearest available area. Keep gear and flaps retracted until you are sure of reaching desired landing spot.

   (d) *If sufficient runway is available*—land straight ahead, regardless of airspeed.

2. **Failure during cruising flight.**

   (a) Increase power on good engine to METO.

   (b) Maintain engine-out best climb speed.

   (c) Reduce power only when unneeded altitude is gained.

(d)   Proceed to a landing at an airport, or the first available area, in accordance with 1(c) above.

3.

Weight and balance

A multiengine pilot should be even more familiar with aircraft weight and balance procedures than the single-engine pilot owing to the greater choice open to the twin-engine pilot. His airplane probably has more baggage compartments, more fuel tanks, and more seats for passengers, and he must be able to select and distribute his load so that the airplane will be within its weight and balance limitation.

It may be simplest to approach weight and balance as two separate items, and therefore weight will be discussed first.

WEIGHT

The difference between the empty weight of the airplane and its maximum gross weight is the useful load. This figure can be determined from the Weight and Balance Data originally furnished with the airplane by the manufacturer (Fig. 4) or from the proper entry in the aircraft log (two samples of which are shown in Fig. 5)

CESSNA S/N ___310G-0008___ **CESSNA AIRCRAFT COMPANY**

Cessna •   **WICHITA, KANSAS**   Cessna •

MODEL 310G

DATE ___14 Dec. 1961___ **WEIGHT AND BALANCE DATA**

N8908Z   (std)
REGISTRATION NUMBER

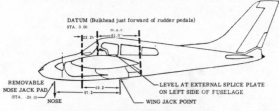

DATUM (Bulkhead just forward of rudder pedals)
STA. 0.00

REMOVABLE NOSE JACK PAD
(STA. -28.0)
NOSE

LEVEL AT EXTERNAL SPLICE PLATE
ON LEFT SIDE OF FUSELAGE
WING JACK POINT

ACTUAL

AIRCRAFT AS WEIGHED

POSITION	SCALE READING	SCALE DRIFT	TARE	NET WEIGHT
LEFT WING	1004.0	+2.0		1006.0
RIGHT WING	1034.0	+2.0		1036.0
NOSE	1138.0	+3.0	-16.0	1125.0
AIRCRAFT TOTAL AS WEIGHED				3167.0

C.G. Arm of Aircraft as Weighed $= (69.2) - \dfrac{(97.2) \times (\overset{\text{Nose Net Weight}}{1125.0})}{(\underset{\text{Total as Weighed}}{3167.0})} = (34.7)$ Inches aft of Datum

NOTE: Because of high standards of quality control during production, it is not necessary to actually weigh every aircraft. Every tenth aircraft is weighed to insure maintenance of quality standards.

LICENSED EMPTY WEIGHT AND C.G.

ITEM		WEIGHT (LBS.)	C.G. ARM (IN.)	MOMENT (LB-IN)
AIRCRAFT (CALCULATED) (AS WEIGHED)		3167.0	34.7	109894.9
UNDRAINABLE OIL		-45.0 / 1.0	-3.5	-157.5 / -3.5
UNUSABLE FUEL	MAIN	12.0	44.0	528.0
	AUX			
PAINT		21.0	86.0	1806.0
TOTAL LICENSED EMPTY WEIGHT		3122.0	35.1	109737.4

ALLOWABLE USEFUL LOAD

LICENSED GROSS WEIGHT	4990 Lbs
SUBTRACT: LICENSED EMPTY WEIGHT	3122 LBS
ALLOWABLE USEFUL LOAD	1868 LBS

IT IS THE RESPONSIBILITY OF THE AIRPLANE OWNER AND THE PILOT TO INSURE THAT THE AIRPLANE IS LOADED PROPERLY. THE EMPTY WEIGHT C.G. AND USEFUL LOAD ARE NOTED ABOVE FOR THIS AIRPLANE AS DELIVERED FROM THE FACTORY. IF THE AIRPLANE HAS BEEN ALTERED, REFER TO THE LATEST APPROVED REPAIR AND ALTERATION FORM (ACA 337) FOR THIS INFORMATION.

Fig. 4—The useful load at the time of the plane's manufacture is shown on the weight and balance data forms provided by the manufacturer.

WEIGHT AND BALANCE DATA

AIRPLANE EMPT. WT.	E. C. G.	NORMAL USEFUL LOAD	UTILITY USEFUL LOAD	DATE	SIGNATURE OF CERTIFICATED MECHANIC OR REPAIR FACILITY

DATE 19__	TOTAL TIME IN SERVICE	CURRENT WEIGHT AND BALANCE INFORMATION			
		EMPTY WEIGHT	EMPTY C. G.	USEFUL LOAD	REMARKS

Fig. 5—Sample pages from two different aircraft logs each with space for entering useful load data.

The useful load is comprised of pilot/s, passengers, fuel, oil, and baggage. These variables must be kept within the weight limit prescribed. The fact that an airplane has five seats, X number of gallons of fuel capacity, and Y number of pounds of maximum baggage capacity does not necessarily mean that the pilot can operate with full fuel, full passenger load, and full baggage load. Instead he must calculate these weights to keep within the useful load. For example, if he must carry full passenger seats, then some of the fuel may have to be sacrificed, while with vacant seats this weight could be used for fuel.

A certain light twin-engine airplane, to cite an example, might have the following specifications:

Maximum gross weight .... 4,800 lbs.
Empty weight .... 3,150 lbs.
Useful load .... 1,650 lbs.
Fuel capacity .... 100 gals. in main tanks, 30 gals. in auxiliary tanks.
Oil capacity .... 6 gallons.
Maximum baggage capacity : 200 lbs.
Seating capacity .... 5 seats.

Were the pilot to attempt to carry full tanks, full seats, and full baggage, the weight would appear as follows:

Fuel: 130 gals. @ 6 lbs. per gal. .... 780 lbs.
Oil: 6 gals. @ 7.5 lbs. per gal. .... 45 lbs.
Pilot and passengers: 5 @ 170 lbs. each ...... 850 lbs.
Baggage .... 200 lbs.

Total 1875 lbs.
Useful Load 1650 lbs.
Overload 225 lbs.

To prevent this, the pilot could leave the 30-gallon auxiliary tanks empty and cut down baggage by 45 pounds. Another option would be to drain $7\frac{1}{2}$ gallons from the main tanks, auxiliary tanks empty, and leave baggage at 200 pounds. Various combinations are open to the pilot, and circumstances will dictate which he uses.

BALANCE

The preceding explanation has shown how to keep the weight within limits, but weight is only half of weight and balance. Because its load of fuel, passengers, and baggage is greater that that of a single-engine airplane, it is more likely for a multiengine airplane to be "out of balance," that is, to have its center of gravity limits exceeded. Therefore, the pilot should have a knowledge of the theory of balance, or center of gravity.

The theory of balance is extremely simple. It is that of the familiar child's see-saw, which is in balance when it rests on its fulcrum in a level position. The influence of weight is directly dependent upon its distance from the fulcrum. A lighter child on the extreme end of the see-saw has the same effect as a heavier child nearer the fulcrum. The distance from the weight to the fulcrum is called the *arm*. The arm multiplied by the weight is called the *moment*.

Similarly, an airplane would be balanced if it remained level when suspended from an imaginary point. This point is its *center of gravity*, or *CG*. The allowable variation of the location of the CG of the airplane is known as its *CG range*; thus we have a forward CG limit and an aft CG limit. Keeping the airplane within the CG limits is accomplished by placing loads so that the average arm of a loaded airplane falls within the CG limits.

The manufacturer designates an arbitrary reference point near the nose of the airplane as the *datum line*. The distance from this datum line to the individual weights (fuel, pilots, passengers, baggage, etc.) is the arm for that weight, and the arm multiplied by the weight gives the moment. All the weights and all the moments are totalled, and dividing the total moment by the total weight gives the average arm, or CG. If the CG falls within the CG limits, the loading is satisfactory.

The manufacturer usually shortens this procedure for the pilot by using graphs and tables to do the multiplica-

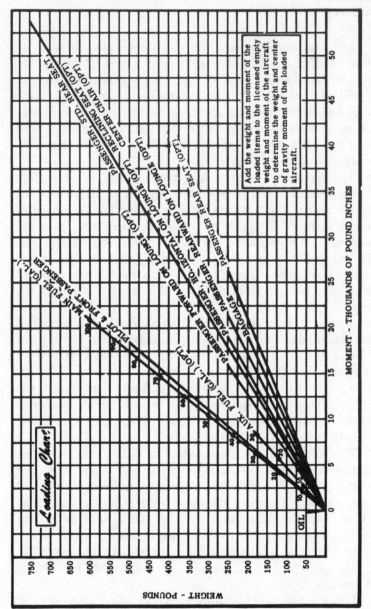

Fig. 6.

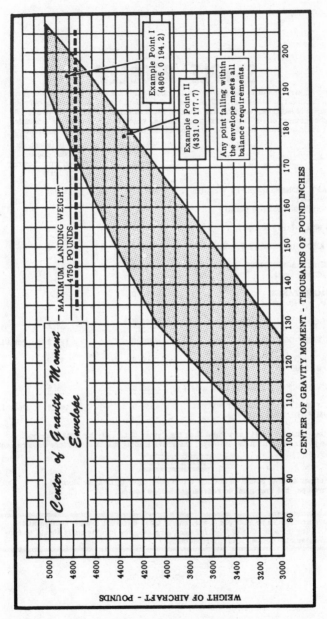

Fig. 7.

SAMPLE PROBLEM

Assume an airplane of the following configuration: Pilot and front seat passenger, three rear seat passengers, 100 gallons fuel in main tanks, 24 quarts of oil and 180 pounds of baggage. Assume this airplane has a licensed empty weight of 3130.0 lbs and a moment of 107.3 thousand pound-inches, which includes 12 lbs of unusable fuel, 1 lb undrainable oil, 21 lbs paint and 71 lbs of optional electronic equipment.

	Weight in pounds	Moment in thousands of pound-inches (Obtained from Loading Chart)	
AIRCRAFT LICENSED EMPTY WEIGHT. . . . AND MOMENT (From weight and balance sheet)	3130.0	107.3	
OIL (24 qts. x 1.875 lb./qt.)	45.0	-0.2	
PILOT AND FRONT SEAT PASSENGER	340.0	12.6	
REAR SEAT PASSENGERS . . . . (Standard rear seat)	510.0	36.2	
FUEL (MAIN TANKS) . . . . (100 gals. x 6 lb./gal.)	600.0	21.0	
BAGGAGE	180.0	17.3	
TOTAL TAKE-OFF WEIGHT	4805.0	194.2	Point I
SUBTRACT TOTAL FUEL . . . . LISTED ABOVE	600.0	21.0	
ADD MINIMUM FUEL RESERVE (21 gals.) . .	126.0	4.5	
TOTAL WEIGHT AND MOMENT WITH . . . . MINIMUM FUEL RESERVE	4331.0	177.7	Point II

Locate the values of Point I and Point II on the Center of Gravity Moment Envelope. Since the points fall within the envelope, the above loading meets all balance requirements.

WARNING

If either or both points do not fall within the Center of Gravity Moment Envelope, the load must be rearranged before takeoff.

The above problem is an example of only one of many different loading configurations. To best utilize the available payload for each airplane, the loading chart should be consulted to determine proper load distribution.

Fig. 8.

tion and division. One manufacturer of light twin-engine aircraft uses the graphs shown in Figs. 6 and 7.

The steps to be followed in working the sample problem in Fig. 8 are as follows:

(1) Write down the weight and moment of the empty airplane as taken from the airplane's Weight and Balance Report (Fig. 4), or from the latest Form 337 (Fig. 5).

(2) Write down the weight of the oil and determine its moment from the Loading Chart (Fig. 6). (The oil is forward of the datum line and thus has a negative moment value.)

(3) Write down the weight of the pilot and front-seat passenger and determine the moment from the Loading Chart. (Locate the weight on the line representing pilot and front-seat passenger and read down to the moment.)

(4) Repeat for rear-seat passengers. (The Loading Chart is performing the function of multiplying the arm by the weight to give the moments, shown in thousands for mathematical convenience.)

(5) Repeat for fuel in the main tanks.

(6) Repeat for baggage.

(7) Add the weights and add the moments. Then locate these figures on the center of gravity moment envelope. These intersect at *Point I* in the example in Fig. 7, and show satisfactory center of gravity location. (This has performed the function of locating the CG by dividing the total moment by the total weight.)

These seven steps have determined the CG for the takeoff weight and loading configuration. The CG for landing, as shown in the sample problem, is determined in a similar manner.

Another manufacturer of light twin-engine airplanes uses tables instead of graphs (see Figs. 9, 9A, and 9B). The loading calculations to be performed by the pilot are as follows:

(1)   Write down the weight and moment of the empty airplane as taken from the airplane's Weight and Balance Report, or from the latest Form 337.

(2)   Write down the weight and moment of oil as taken from the table for oil in the schedule of Useful Load Weights and Moments. (The tables multiply the weight by the arm to give the moments, which are divided by 100 for mathematical convenience.)

(3)   Write down the weight and moment of fuel in the main tanks. (In the example, the tanks are filled to 88 gallons. This is multiplied by 6 in the tables to give the weight—528—and this in turn is multiplied by the arm to give the moment—734.)

(4)   Repeat the above step for all useful-load items.

BEECHCRAFT E50 TWIN-BONANZA WEIGHT AND BALANCE USEFUL LOAD WEIGHTS AND MOMENTS (OPTIONAL SEATING ARRANGEMENT)

SAMPLE LOADING CALCULATION

	Weight	Moment 100
Empty Weight	4536	5167
Oil	60	62
Fuel—Main	528	734
—Auxiliary	600	774
Anti-Icer Fluid	0	0
Pilot and Front Passenger	340	394
Rear Passengers—Chair	170	269
—Couch	340	505
Baggage—Front	126	76
—Rear	300	579
Total at Takeoff	7000	8460
Use Fuel for Two Hours' Flight—Main Tank	−360	−500
Total After Two Hours' Flight	6640	7960
Use Fuel for Remainder of Flight—Auxiliary Tank	−600	−774
Total at Landing	6040	7186

Fig. 9.

BEECHCRAFT E50 TWIN-BONANZA
WEIGHT AND BALANCE
CENTER OF GRAVITY TABLE

Weight	Minimum Moment 100	Maximum Moment 100
6010	6948	4788
6020	6961	7501
6030	6974	7513
6040	6987	7526
6050	7000	7538
6060	7013	7551
6070	7026	7563
6960	8206	8672
6970	8220	8685
6980	8233	8697
6990	8247	8710
7000	8260	8722

FUEL

MAIN WING TANKS			TWO 71-GAL. AUXILIARY WING TANKS		
Gals.	Weight	Moment 100	Gals.	Weight	Moment 100
5	30	42	5	30	39
10	60	83	10	60	77
15	90	125	15	90	116
20	120	167	20	120	155
25	150	209	25	150	194
30	180	250	30	180	232
35	210	292	35	210	271
40	240	334	40	240	310
45	270	375	45	270	348
50	300	417	50	300	387
55	330	459	55	330	426
60	360	500	60	360	464
65	390	542	65	390	503
70	420	584	70	420	542
75	450	626	75	450	581
80	480	667	80	480	619
85	510	709	85	510	658
88	528	734	90	540	697
			95	570	735
			100	600	774

Fig. 9A.

OCCUPANTS

FRONT SEATS		REAR CHAIRS	
Weight	Moment 100	Weight	Moment 100
120	139	120	190
130	151	130	205
140	162	140	221
150	174	150	237
160	186	160	253
170	197	170	269
180	209	180	284
190	220	190	300
200	232	200	316

REAR COUCH

Weight	Forward Moment 100	Mid Moment 100	Aft Moment 100
120	167	190	212
130	181	205	230
140	195	221	248
150	209	237	266
160	222	253	283
170	236	269	301
180	250	284	319
190	264	300	336
200	278	316	354

BAGGAGE

FORWARD		REAR	
Weight	Moment 100	Weight	Moment 100
10	6	10	19
20	12	20	39
30	18	30	58
40	24	40	77
50	30	50	97
60	36	60	116
70	42	70	135
80	48	80	154
90	54	90	174
100	60	100	193
110	66	110	212
120	72	120	232
130	78	130	251
140	84	140	270
150	90	150	290
160	96	160	309
170	102	170	328
180	108	180	347
190	114	190	367
200	120	200	386
		210	405
		220	425
		230	444
		240	463
		250	483
		260	502
		270	521
		280	540
		290	560
		300	579

PROP. ANTI-ICER FLUID

Gals.	Weight	Moment 100
3	20	23

OIL

Gals.	Weight	Moment 100
8	60	62

Fig. 9B.

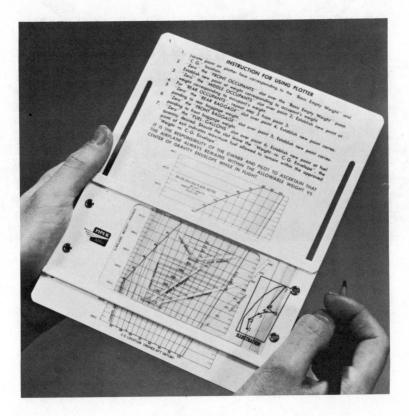

Fig. 10—Weight and balance plotter. *(Piper Aircraft Corp.)*

(5)   Add the weights and add the moments. Locate
      the weight in the Center of Gravity Table, and
      check to see if the moment falls within the mini-
      mum and maximum moments shown for that
      weight.

These steps have determined the CG for takeoff. The
CG after two hours of flight and the CG for landing are
found in a similar manner, as shown in the example.

Still another manufacturer of light twins makes a
weight and balance plotter which can be used for compu-
tations in loading (see Fig. 10).

Beechcraft King Air.

4.

The flight test (class rating)

This chapter contains the FAA's own published guidelines to the actual flight test for the multiengine rating, together with some practical hints and advice from the author of this manual for meeting the requirements of that test. The material is designed (1) to provide the student with information that will enable him to take full advantage of the extra safety inherent in multiengine airplanes, and (2) to inform the experienced multiengine pilot of the specific maneuvers and performance standards required by the revised Part 61 of the FAR's for a class rating. (FAA guidelines to the flight test for the *type* rating are included in Chapt. 7 of this manual.)

(The following material is from *Flight Test Guide, Multiengine Airplane Class and Type Ratings, FAA Publication AC 61-57.*)

GENERAL INFORMATION

Part 61 of the Federal Aviation Regulations has been revised and upgraded to reflect the complexity of the modern aircraft as well as its operating environment. In the past, airman certification requirements could be met by training a student to pass a written test and then to demonstrate his ability to perform predetermined flight training maneuvers during a flight test. Rather than merely duplicating on the flight test the maneuvers used for training, the new training and certification concept requires that the applicant for a multiengine class or type rating receive instruction in and demonstrate his competency in all pilot operations listed in pertinent sections of this guide. A pilot operation, as used in this guide, is a group of related procedures and maneuvers involving skills and knowledge required to safely and efficiently function as a pilot. The specific procedures and maneuvers used to teach the pilot operations are listed in Part 61 (revised). Instead, the instructor is permitted to select procedures and maneuvers from FAA approved training publications pertinent to the certificate or rating sought. The instructor indicates by written statement that the applicant has demonstrated competency in all the required pilot operations and considers him qualified to pass the flight test. On the class and type rating flight tests, the examiner selects the procedures and maneuvers to be performed by the applicant to show competency in each required pilot operation.

Use of this guide

This guide contains an *Objective* for each required pilot operation. Under each pilot operation, pertinent procedures of maneuvers are listed with *Descriptions* and *Acceptable performance guidelines.*

1. The *Objective* states briefly the purpose of each pilot operation required on the flight test.

2. The *Description* provides information on what may be asked of the applicant regarding the selected procedure or maneuver. The procedures or maneuvers listed have been found most effective in demonstrating the objective of that particular pilot operation.

3. The *Acceptable performance guidelines* include the factors which will be taken into account by the examiner in deciding whether the applicant has met the objective of the pilot operation. The airspeed, altitude, and heading tolerances given represent the minimum performance expected in good flying conditions. However, consistently exceeding these tolerances before corrective action is initiated is indicative of an unsatisfactory performance. Any procedure or action, or the

lack thereof, which requires the intervention of the examiner to maintain safe flight will be disqualifying. Failure to take positive action to ensure that the flight area is clear of conflicting traffic will also be disqualifying.

The applicant's performance will be evaluated on the basis of the judgment, knowledge, accuracy, and smoothness he displays on the flight test. A competent performance is one in which the pilot is obviously the master of the airplane and the successful completion of the procedure or maneuver is never seriously in doubt.

Emphasis will be placed on the procedures and maneuvers which are most critical to a safe performance as a multiengine pilot. Spatial disorientation, collision avoidance, and wake turbulence hazards will also be emphasized. The applicant will be expected to know the meaning and significance of the airplane performance speeds important to a multiengine pilot, and be able to readily find the speeds appropriate to the airplane used for the flight test. These speeds include at least:

V_{so} —the stalling speed or minimum steady flight speed in landing configuration.

V_{le} —the maximum landing gear extended speed.

V_{fe} —the maximum flap-extended speed.

V_y —the speed for the best rate-of-climb with all engines operating.

V_x —the speed for the best angle-of-climb with all engines operating.

V_a —the design maneuvering speed.

V_{ne} —the never-exceed speed.

V_{mc}—the minimum control speed with critical engine inoperative.

V_1 —the critical engine failure speed.

V_2 —the takeoff safety speed.

General procedures for flight tests

The ability of an applicant for an aircraft class or type rating to perform the required pilot operations is based on the following:

1. Executing procedures and maneuvers within the aircraft's performance capabilities and limitations, including use of the aircraft's systems.

2. Executing emergency procedures and maneuvers appropriate to the aircraft.

3. Piloting the aircraft with smoothness and accuracy.

4. Exercising judgment.

5. Applying his aeronautical knowledge.

6. Showing that he is the master of the aircraft, with the successful outcome of a procedure or maneuver never seriously in doubt.

If the applicant fails any of the required pilot operations, he fails the flight test. The examiner or the applicant may discontinue the test at any time when the failure of a required pilot operation makes the applicant ineligible for the certificate or rating sought. If the test is discontinued, the applicant is entitled to credit for only those entire pilot operations that he has successfully performed.

I. PREFLIGHT OPERATIONS

Objective. To determine that the applicant has the knowledge and ability to determine that the airplane is airworthy and ready for safe flight.

A. Airplane performance and systems operations

1. Description. The applicant may be asked to use the manufacturer's published recommendations (FAA approved Airplane Flight Manual material when such material has been approved for the airplane type or other manufacturer's published recommendations such as "Owner's Manual," or "Owner's Handbook") to determine the effects of such factors as temperature, density altitude, wind, surface conditions, and gross weight on flight performance. He should be familiar with the effects of power settings and altitude on the cruising range, and know the airspeeds for best performance in the airplane used. Special attention should be devoted to the performance data on flight control and performance with an engine inoperative. He should also have a practical knowledge of the flight control system; the fuel, lubrication, hydraulic, and electrical systems; the operation of the superchargers, landing gear and flaps, radio, pressurization, heating and ventilation installations; and of fire control, deicing, antiicing, and other emergency equipment appropriate to the type of airplane used.

2. *Acceptable performance guidelines.* The applicant shall determine and explain the performance capabilities, approved operating procedures, and limitations for the airplane used, as well as the power settings, placarded speeds, range, fuel and oil requirements, the operation of aircraft systems and special equipment, critical engine-out control speeds and climb speeds, and other emergency procedures. The inability to obtain essential pilot information which is available for the airplane, or the incorrect use of this information, shall be disqualifying.

B. Airplane loading

1. *Description.* The applicant may be asked to determine that the airplane loading is within limits. He should use current and approved weight and balance data to make a practical computation of the permissible load distribution including fuel, oil, passengers, and baggage as appropriate to the flight proposed.

2. *Acceptable performance guidelines.* The applicant shall make accurate determinations of gross weight and load distribution. A loading graph or computer designed for the airplane may be used for this purpose.

C. Airplane line Check

1. *Description.* The applicant may be asked to check the airplane's readiness for flight, including fuel and oil supply, the presence of all required equipment and documents, and its airworthiness so far as can be determined by visual inspection. A checklist provided by the manufacturer or operator should be used.

2. *Acceptable performance guidelines.* The applicant shall use an orderly procedure in conducting a preflight check of the airplane. He shall know the significance of each item checked and the appropriate remedial action for the pilot to initiate for the correction of each unsatisfactory item detected. Failure to recognize any obvious unairworthy condition shall be disqualifying.

D. Engine starting and pretakeoff operational checks

1. *Description.* The applicant may be asked to demon-

strate engine starting and pretakeoff operational checks of the airplane systems and equipment, flight controls, and engine runup. A checklist provided by the manufacturer or operator should be used.

2. Acceptable performance guidelines. The applicant shall use an orderly procedure in starting engines and performing pretakeoff operational checks. He shall know the significance of each item checked and the appropriate remedial action for a pilot to initiate for the correction of each unsatisfactory item detected. Failure to recognize any obvious unairworthy condition shall be disqualifying.

II. AIRPORT OPERATIONS

Objective. To determine that the applicant can maneuver multiengine landplanes or seaplanes safely and expeditiously on the surface and in flight in conformance with published procedures or Air Traffic Control instructions.

A. Taxiing (landplanes)

1. Description. The applicant may be asked to demonstrate taxiing at speeds appropriate to the area of operations. He should determine that the taxi path is clear of obstructions and comply with local taxi rules or control tower instructions as appropriate.

2. Acceptable performance guidelines. The applicant shall taxi the airplane accurately, safely, and with consideration for other aircraft and personnel on ramps and taxiways; and shall properly use differential power, brakes, and flight controls for directional control; and shall operate nosewheel steering and tailwheel lock, if the airplane is so equipped.

B. Taxiing (seaplanes)

1. Description. The applicant may be asked to demonstrate taxiing at slow speeds and on the step, into the wind, downwind, and crosswind. Turns to downwind headings, step turns, sailing, docking, and simulated or actual approaches to a buoy should be included. The applicant should demonstrate the use of differential power and, if the seaplane is so equipped, taxiing with and without the use of water rudder.

2. Acceptable Performance Guidelines. The applicant's competence in taxiing shall be evaluated on the basis of his proper use of flight controls, differential power, and water rudder to safely and effectively maneuver the seaplane. Any faulty technique which results in a hazardous situation shall be disqualifying.

C. Collision avoidance precautions

1. Description. The applicant is expected to exercise conscientious and continuous surveillance of the airspace in which the airplane is being operated to guard against potential mid-air collisions. In addition to "see and avoid" practices, he is expected to use VFR Advisory Service at nonradar facilities, Airport Advisory Service at non-tower airports or FSS locations, and Radar Traffic Information Service, where available.

2. Acceptable performance guidelines. The applicant shall maintain continuous vigilance for other aircraft and take immediate actions necessary to avoid any situation which could result in a mid-air collision. Extra precautions shall be taken, particularly in areas of congested traffic, to ensure that his view of other aircraft is not obstructed by his aircraft's structure. When traffic advisory service is used, the applicant shall understand terminology used by the radar controller in reporting positions of other aircraft. Failure to maintain proper surveillance shall be disqualifying.

D. Wake turbulence avoidance

1. Description. The applicant may be asked to explain wingtip vortices, their characteristics and associated hazards. He should follow the recommended courses of action to remain clear of wake turbulence.

2. Acceptable Performance Guidelines. The applicant shall identify the conditions and locations in which wake turbulence may be encountered and adjust his flight path in a manner to avoid those areas. Failure to follow recommended courses of action for minimizing the possibility of flying into wingtip vortices shall be disqualifying.

III. TAKEOFFS AND LANDINGS

Objective. To determine that the applicant is competent in performing takeoffs and landings in landplanes or seaplanes under all normally anticipated conditions.

A. Normal and crosswind takeoffs and landings (landplanes)

 1. Description. The applicant may be requested to demonstrate normal and crosswind takeoffs and landings. For safety, crosswind takeoffs and landings should be performed with full consideration for other air traffic, and in strict compliance with the crosswind limitations for landings in the airplane used. Takeoffs and landings at various flap settings, including a no-flap landing if permitted by the airplane's operating limitations, should be included. *Note:* If wind conditions are such that a crosswind technique is required for each takeoff and landing, a separate crosswind demonstration will not be required.

 2. Acceptable performance guidelines. The applicant shall perform takeoffs and landings in accordance with the procedures and instructions in the manufacturer's published recommendations. He shall maintain a straight ground track on the takeoff and landing roll. Lift-off, climb, approach, and touchdown speeds shall be appropriate for existing conditions. The applicant shall observe the crosswind limitations of the airplane used.

B. Maximum performance takeoffs and landings (landplanes)

 1. Description. The applicant may be asked to demonstrate a short field takeoff. He should initiate lift-off just below the all-engine best angle-of-climb speed, unless it is slower than the engine-out minimum control speed, in which case the engine-out minimum control speed should be used. The best all-engine angle-of-climb speed should be attained and maintained to the height of an assumed obstruction, after which normal climb speed should be smoothly attained. He may be asked to demonstrate short field landings made from a normal traffic pattern. Full flaps should be used for the last segment of the approach. Moderate slips may also be used. The applicant should not steepen his approach slope after crossing the assumed obstruction. The flare for touchdown should result in little or no floating after the throttle is closed.

 2. Acceptable performance guidelines. Performance shall be evaluated on the basis of the applicant's takeoff and landing technique, judgment, observance of traffic patterns and control tower instructions, drift correction, coordination, and smoothness. Excessive maneuvering, faulty operation of aircraft controls or systems, climbing at less than engine-out minimum control speed, or the use of improper approach speeds shall be disqualifying.

C. Rejected landing (landplanes)

1. Description. The applicant may be instructed to go-around from a point just prior to touchdown in landing configuration. The execution of a go-around with a simulated engine failure will not be required.

2. Acceptable performance guidelines. The applicant shall maintain positive airplane control and appropriate airspeeds, operate the flaps and gear in proper sequence, and use correct power and trim settings. Climbing higher than necessary to clear immediate obstructions at less than the minimum engine-out control speed shall be disqualifying.

D. Normal and crosswind takeoffs (seaplanes)

1. Description. The applicant may be requested to demonstrate takeoffs into the wind, and with light crosswind components. He may also be asked to demonstrate, when feasible, or to describe in detail any or all of the following: (a) high density altitude takeoffs from glassy water; (b) takeoffs from choppy water or ocean swells; and (c) takeoffs from streams or inlets with significant current or tide and downstream wind.

2. Acceptable performance guidelines. The applicant's performance shall be evaluated on the basis of his smooth operation of the power and flight controls, his directional control, and his ability to achieve an efficient planing attitude promptly and to make a smooth, effective transition to flight. Misuse of the controls, consistent retarding of takeoffs by premature rotation for liftoff, or failure to take immediate corrective action to stop porpoising while on the step shall be disqualifying.

E. Normal and crosswind landings (seaplanes)

1. Description. The applicant may be asked to demonstrate landings into the wind, and with light crosswind components. Landing approaches should be made in accordance with the established traffic pattern for the area used, and with a final approach speed of approximately 1.3 times the power-off stalling speed in landing configuration (1.3 Vso;, or the final approach speed recommended by the aircraft manufacturer. A straight course should be maintained during touchdown and throughout the runout on the surface. The applicant may also be asked to demonstrate, if feasible, or to describe in detail, any of the following: (a) landings on glassy water; (b) landings on choppy water or ocean swells, and (c) emergency landings on airports or unprepared fields.

2. *Acceptable performance guidelines.* The applicant's performance shall be evaluated on the basis of the accuracy of his approaches, correction for wind drift, correct use of the controls in flight and on the surface, and landing technique. He shall maintain the desired final approach speed within plus or minus 5 knots, and touch down smoothly within the area specified by the examiner.

IV. FLIGHT AT CRITICALLY SLOW AIRSPEEDS AND INCREASED LOAD FACTORS

Objective. To determine that the applicant is competent in controlling the airplane at minimum flight airspeeds and under changing load factors.

A. Maneuvering at Minimum Controllable Airspeed

1. *Description.* The applicant may be requested to maneuver the airplane at an airspeed not more than 10 knots above the stalling speed in cruise and landing configurations. This includes transition from and to cruising configuration and airspeed in straight-and-level flight.

2. *Acceptable performance guidelines.* The applicant shall be able to maneuver the airplane at minimum controllable airspeed, maintain a speed within plus or minus five knots of the desired airspeed, and maintain an altitude within plus or minus one hundred feet of the assigned altitude. In straight-and-level flight, and during the transition to and from the minimum controllable airspeed, he shall maintain a heading within plus or minus 10° of the original heading. The applicant shall use proper trim and power settings for existing conditions. Any unintentional stall shall be disqualifying.

B. Imminent stalls

1. *Description.* The applicant may be asked to demon-

strate the recognition of and recovery from stalls, with and without power, in landing and cruising configuration, from straight and turning flight, climbs, and glides. (No stall will be required with any engine throttled or cut off and the other engine(s) developing effective power. Abrupt pitch changes during stall demonstrations, and all other maneuvers, should be avoided in airplanes with extensions between the engine and the propeller, because of the high gyroscopic loads induced.)

2. Acceptable performance guidelines. The applicant shall use prompt and correct control applications to achieve the desired attitudes and maintain the desired heading. Stall recoveries shall be accomplished positively and smoothly, with coordinated flight control usage, the smooth application of power, and the least loss of altitude consistent with the prompt recovery of control effectiveness. Failure to initiate corrective action on imminent stalls before the nose pitches uncontrollably, indications of a secondary stall during recoveries, or reaching higher than cruising airspeed during recoveries shall be disqualifying.

C. Steep turns
1. Description. The applicant may be asked to execute turns maintaining a constant altitude and angle of bank at least 45°, continuing for 360° or more of turn.

2. Acceptable performance guidelines. The applicant shall maintain an altitude within plus or minus 100 feet of the entry altitude, airspeed within plus or minus 10 knots of that assigned, and a bank with less than 10° of variation after the turn is established, and complete recoveries within plus or minus 10° of the assigned headings. The applicant shall use smooth, coordinated flight control applications, and maintain orientation throughout the turns.

V. INSTRUMENT FLIGHT

Objective. To determine that the applicant is competent in controlling and maneuvering the airplane solely by reference to flight instruments.

A. Normal maneuvers and recovery from unusual flight attitudes

This paragraph applies to the applicant for the multiengine airplane class rating who does *not* hold an instrument rating (airplane). It also applies to the applicant for a multiengine airplane type rating who does *not* hold or is *not* concurrently obtaining an instrument rating (airplane).

1. Description. The applicant may be asked to perform normal flight maneuvers and recovery from unusual flight attitudes solely by reference to flight instruments. This should be accomplished using full flight instrumentation if available. However, it may be accomplished using only a gyroscopic rate of turn indicator and a sensitive altimeter in addition to the usual VFR instruments. Any control or stability augmentation system (partial or full autopilot) should be rendered inoperative unless it is required equipment for the airplane used.

Flight maneuvers for this demonstration may be selected from the following: (a) recovery from the start of a power-on spiral; (b) recovery from the approach to a climbing stall; (c) normal turns of at least 180° left and right to within plus or minus 20° of a preselected heading; (d) shallow climbing turns to a preselected altitude; (e) shallow descending turns at reduced power to a preselected altitude; and (f) straight and level flight.

2. Acceptable performance guidelines. The applicant shall control the airplane solely by reference to flight instruments. He shall use smooth and coordinated flight control applications. Any loss of control which makes it necessary for the examiner to take control to avoid a stall or exceeding the operating limitations of the airplane used shall be disqualifying.

B. Instrument flight rules operations

This paragraph applies to the applicant for the multiengine airplane class rating who holds an instrument rating (airplane).

1. Description. The applicant may be asked to perform normal flight maneuvers and recovery from unusual attitudes while operating the airplane under simulated instrument conditions. Performance of the following procedures and maneuvers solely by reference to flight instruments may be accomplished: (a) recovery from unusual flight attitudes including approaches to stalls; (b) a standard instrument approach; (c) maneuvering with one engine inoperative—propeller feathered or power reduced to simulate the drag of a feathered propeller; and (d) instrument emergencies.

2. *Acceptable performance guidelines.* The standards for the performance of these procedures and maneuvers shall be in accordance with those in AC 61-56, Instrument Pilot Airplane Flight Test Guide.

VI. EMERGENCY PROCEDURES

Objective. To determine that the applicant can use the correct procedures to effectively and safely cope with emergencies in a multiengine airplane.

A. Maneuvering with one engine inoperative

1. *Description.* The applicant may be asked to demonstrate engine shutdown procedures and flight with one engine inoperative (propeller feathered, if possible). This includes straight-and-level flight and 20° to 30° banked turns toward and away from the inoperative engine. Also included are descents to prescribed altitudes and, in airplanes which are capable of climbing under the existing conditions, climbs to prescribed altitudes.

Note: The feathering of one propeller should be required on a flight test in any multiengine airplane equipped with propellers which can be safely feathered and unfeathered in flight. Feathering for pilot test purposes should be required only under such conditions and at such altitudes and positions where safe landings on established airports can be readily accomplished in the event difficulty is encountered in unfeathering.

If the airplane used is not equipped with propellers which can be safely feathered and unfeathered in flight, the applicant may be asked to shut down one engine in flight in accordance with the procedures in the manufacturer's published recommendations. The regulations do not specifically require an applicant to unfeather a propeller on a flight test. Accordingly, he is not required to do so if he elects to land with a propeller feathered. If he desires to use this procedure, he should arrange it in advance with the examiner concerned, who will permit it unless he considers that an undue hazard would be involved.

2. *Acceptable performance guidelines.* The applicant shall use prescribed propeller operating procedures as well as the recommended emergency settings of all ignition, fuel, electrical, hydraulic, and fire extinguishing systems appropriate to an engine failure. He shall maintain his heading within plus or minus 20° of the original heading during the feathering and unfeathering procedures, and his altitude within plus or minus 100 feet of the original altitude if it is within the capability of the airplane used; he shall promptly identify the inoperative engine after a simulated power failure; and use accurate shutdown and restart procedures, as prescribed in the manufacturer's published recommendations. In an airplane not capable of maintaining altitude with an engine inoperative under existing circumstances, the applicant shall maintain an airspeed within plus or minus 5 knots of the engine-out best rate-of-climb speed and shall use prescribed operating procedures and proper trim settings.

B. **Engine-out minimum control speed demonstration**

1. *Description.* The applicant may be asked to demonstrate airplane controllability problems associated with attempted flight with one engine inoperative at less than minimum engine-out control speed (Vmc), recognition of imminent loss of control and application of proper recovery techniques.

Note: There is a density altitude above which the stalling speed is higher than the engine-out minimum control speed. When this density altitude exists close to the ground because of high elevations or temperatures, an effective flight demonstration is impossible and should not be attempted. When a flight demonstration is impossible, the significance of the engine-out minimum control speed should be emphasized on the oral, including the results of attempting engine-out flight at below this speed, the recognition of imminent loss of control, and recovery techniques.

2. *Acceptable performance guidelines.* The applicant shall demonstrate a complete and accurate knowledge of the cause, effect, and significance of the engine-out minimum control speed, of the clues to be watched for by the pilot, and the safe recovery procedures. The engine-out minimum control

speed flight demonstration is subject to so much variation because of differences in airplane flight characteristics, circumstances of flight, and density altitude that definite performance standards cannot be prescribed. The basic criteria are the prompt recognition of imminent loss of control and the prompt initiation of correct recovery actions. An attempt at any time during the flight test to continue level or climbing flight with an engine out at less than the engine-out minimum control speed, except as necessary for this demonstration, shall be disqualifying.

C. Use of engine-out best rate-of-climb speed

1. Description. The applicant may be asked to establish and maintain the best possible rate of climb (or minimum rate of sink) with one engine throttled to simulate the drag of a feathered propeller, or with a propeller feathered by mutual agreement between the applicant and the examiner.

2. Acceptable performance guidelines. The applicant shall determine (from the manufacturer's published recommendations) and shall maintain the prescribed engine-out best rate-of-climb speed. He shall maintain a climb within plus or minus 5 knots of the best rate-of-climb speed and within plus or minus 10° of the desired heading.

D. Effects of airplane configuration on engine-out performance

1. Description. The applicant may be asked to demonstrate the effects of various configurations on engine-out performance. This includes the results of the extension of the landing gear, the flaps, and both; the application of carburetor heat on the operating engine(s); and windmilling of the inoperative engine.

2. Acceptable performance guidelines. The applicant shall maintain an airspeed within plus or minus 5 knots of the best rate-of-climb speed and a heading within plus or minus 10° of the assigned heading while controlling the airplane in the various configurations.

E. Engine failure on takeoff

1. Description. The applicant may be asked to demonstrate engine failure procedures during takeoff operations. After giving due consideration to the airplane's characteristics, runway length, surface conditions, wind direction and velocity, and any other factors which may affect safety, the examiner may, at least once during the flight test, throttle an engine on takeoff, and expect the applicant to proceed as he would in the event of an actual power failure.

Note: If it has been determined that the engine-out rate of climb will not be at least 50 feet per minute at 1,000 feet above the airport, the engine failure should be simulated at a point on the takeoff roll which will permit the airplane to be safely stopped on the remaining portion of the runway.

The feathering of the propeller and securing of the throttled engine should be simulated to keep it available for immediate use, but all other settings should be made as in the case of an actual power failure.

2. *Acceptable performance guidelines.* If it has been determined that the engine-out rate of climb under existing circumstances is at least 50 feet per minute at 1,000 feet above the airport, and he has attained at least the engine-out best angle-of-climb speed when the engine is throttled, the applicant shall continue his takeoff with one engine throttled. If the airspeed is *below* the engine-out best angle-of-climb speed and the landing gear has *not* been retracted, the takeoff shall be abandoned immediately. If the best angle-of-climb speed has been obtained and the landing gear is in the retract cycle, the applicant shall climb out at the engine-out best angle-of-climb speed to clear any obstructions, and thereafter stabilize the airspeed at the engine-out best rate-of-climb speed while cleaning up the airplane and resetting all appropriate systems.

F. Engine-out approach and landing

1. *Description.* The applicant may be asked to make an approach and landing with one engine inoperative. In the event the applicant has elected to land with a propeller feathering, no further demonstration should be required. Otherwise, the landing may be made with an engine throttled to simulate the drag of a feathered propeller or, if feathering propellers are not installed, with an engine throttled to idling. The approach should be continued to a normal landing, and a go-around with an engine out will not be performed unless there is an actual emergency.

2. *Acceptable performance guidelines.* The applicant shall use the correct procedures for the operation of the airplane systems, use appropriate trim settings, observe the regular traffic pattern or approach path, maintain airspeed and aircraft control during touchdown and landing roll. Any reduction of airspeed below the engine-out minimum control speed before the landing flare is initiated shall be disqualifying.

G. Emergency operations

1. *Description.* The applicant may be asked to demonstrate the emergency operation of the retractable gear, flaps, and electrical, fuel, deicing, and hydraulic systems if operationally practical. Emergency operations such as the use of CO_2 pressure for gear extension, or the discharge of a pressure fire extinguisher system should be simulated only. On flight tests in pressurized airplanes, this demonstration should include an emergency descent as might be necessitated by a loss of pressurization. The descent should be initiated and stabilized but no prolonged descent is required. The airspeed or Mach number for the demonstration of an emergency descent should be approximately 10% less than the airplane's structural limitation, to provide a safety margin. When a Mach limitation is the controlling factor at operational altitudes for the airplane used, the descent should be arranged, if practicable, to require the transition from the observance of the Mach limitation to an airspeed limitation. A simulated emergency descent through or near clouds is prohibited.

2. *Acceptable performance guidelines.* The applicant shall respond to emergency situations in accordance with procedures prescribed by the manufacturer's published recommendations. The applicant's performance shall be evaluated on the basis of his knowledge of the emergency procedures for the airplane used, the judgment displayed, and the accuracy of his operations.

(*End of reprinted material from FAA Publication AC 61-57 on flight test requirements for the class rating.*)

HINTS FOR PASSING THE FLIGHT TEST

I. Preflight operations

A. Airplane performance and systems operations. The applicant must study the Operator's Manual, Handbook, or Airplane Flight Manual thoroughly to be able to have the knowledge required in this item, and he should be familiar with all the performance graphs of the airplane (see Chapt. 8). Common weaknesses of the applicant are unfamiliarity with cross-feed operation of the fuel system, vagueness about emergency operation of landing gear, and uncertainty as to what systems may be affected in case of engine failure. For example, some airplanes have hydraulic pumps on the left engine only, and failure of the left engine would mean all hydraulic pressure would have to be obtained by manual pumping.

B. Airplane loading. A common failure of the applicant is to assume that the empty weight of a sample airplane in the Pilot's Handbook is the same for all airplanes and thus applies to his specific airplane, whereas this information must be obtained from one of three places—the Weight and Balance Report, Form 337, or Aircraft Log Book. Care must be taken to use the most recent computation.

C. Airplane line check. One common error is not knowing where to drain all of the fuel sumps. Another is being unable to locate the static source, and some applicants do not know whether or not their airplane has pitot heat and alternate static source.

D. Engine starting and pretakeoff operational checks. Some applicants run the checklist hurriedly, missing one or more items. The applicant should take his time, running the checklist meticulously. Also, a surprising number of applicants are unfamiliar with the "hot start" or "flooded start" procedure for their airplane. What can be more embarrassing than being unable to start the engines right at the outset?

II.   Airport operations

A. Taxiing. The most prevalent fault is "riding" the brakes. Some applicants have never been shown the proper

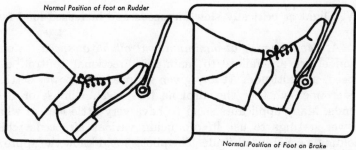

Normal Position of foot on Rudder

Normal Position of Foot on Brake

position of the feet upon the rudder pedals, and consequently, place the feet too high on the pedals and "drag" the brakes through all ground operations. See accompanying figure for proper positioning of feet on rudder pedals.

C. Collision avoidance precautions. At uncontrolled airports, where the chances of mid-air collision are higher, applicant needs to be alert in the traffic pattern, especially (1) on final approach, for aircraft converging from a closer-in base leg, and (2) when on base leg himself, for aircraft on a farther-out final.

D. Wake turbulence avoidance. In spite of all the wealth of information about wake turbulence, a small number of applicants seem unfamiliar with the danger areas.

III. Takeoffs and landings

A. & B. Normal, crosswind, and maximum performance takeoffs and landings. Probably the most common takeoff error is failure to leave the airplane on the ground until it reaches Vmc. A cose second is inattention to the proper climb speeds immediately after takeoff, with many pilots allowing the airspeed to build up excessively, thus sacrificing climb performance. Altitude is more important after takeoff than excess airspeed, and airspeed should be held at best rate-of-climb speed for the first few hundred feet. Of course, if obstacles are ahead, best angle-of-climb speed should be held until obstacles are cleared.

C. Rejected landing. The most prevalent fault is inattention to the appropriate airspeeds.

IV. Flight at critically slow airspeeds and increased load factors

A. Maneuvering at minimum controllable airspeed. Common errors are failure to maintain directional control, airspeed, and altitude. At any given airspeed, the power setting determines whether the airplane flies level, climbs, or descends. Many applicants seem to have very little idea of what power settings to use in producing various airspeeds while holding a constant altitude. The pilot should know the approximate airspeeds that will result from different power settings.

B. Imminent stalls. Some applicants recover prematurely, initiating recovery at the first "beep" from the stall warning indicator. Others dive the aircraft excessively, and still others move the control wheel abruptly, inducing a secondary stall. The ideal maneuver is well described in the *Flight Test Guide.*

C. Steep turns. The most common error is failure to hold altitude. The tendency of the pilot to climb in a right turn is exaggerated in multiengine aircraft because of the wider cabin. In a right turn the pilot is sitting on top of the turn looking down at the nose, and he tends to pull the nose up unnecessarily. In a left turn he has the opposite reaction since he is sitting below the longitudinal axis; in looking up at the nose he considers it high enough, uses insufficient back elevator pressure, and consequently dives around the turn. The pilot must counteract this effect by learning to use a point on the nose directly ahead of his eyes as his visual reference rather than the center of the nose cowling. The artificial horizon and sensitive altimeter can be of great benefit to the student in helping him to determine the proper visual reference, as well as in the actual performance of the turn.

V. Instrument Flight

Formerly, an instrument flight demonstration was not required of an applicant for a multiengine *class* rating, but only for *type* ratings. However, the revised Part 61 requires a demonstration of instrument flight, and this should not be overlooked in the preparation for the test. The applicant should be prepared to demonstrate instrument proficiency as follows:

If he does *not* have an instrument rating, he must demonstrate approximately the same basic instrument maneuvers as those required on a private pilot flight test. Engine-out procedures under the hood are not required. An applicant who *has* an instrument rating must demonstrate maneuvering with an engine inoperative, a standard instrument approach, and recovery from unusual attitudes.

VI. Emergency procedures

A. *Maneuvering with one engine inoperative.* The worst thing the applicant can do here is to feather the wrong engine, and a minority manage to do exactly that. It is an understatement to say that it is far better to take a few seconds longer to feather the proper engine than it is to feather the wrong engine in record time. Occasionally the examiner will encounter an applicant who has never feathered an engine. The applicant should refer to Section VI-A of the *Flight Test Guide,* and, unless feathering is prohibited by its provisions, should have his instructor take him through the feathering procedure until he is proficient.

B. *Engine-out minimum control speed demonstration.* Do not attempt this demonstration with dead engine feathered, but the dead engine should be throttled back to windmilling. The operating engine should be developing maximum power, and the applicant should slowly increase pitch attitude until the aircraft can no longer be held with full rudder and with no more than 5° of bank. At first indication of uncontrollable yaw, pitch should be decreased and power reduced on the operating engine. Control will be regained immediately, and power may be applied as soon as the aircraft is above Vmc. Should the aircraft stall before the loss of directional control, applicant should lower the nose and recover from the stall. This demonstration can be entered easily if the applicant reduces power on both engines, slowly brings the aircraft to the takeoff pitch attitude, and then with airspeed about 10 mph above Vmc closes the throttle on the critical engine and slowly advances the throttle on the operating engine to maximum power. Airspeed should then be reduced by raising the nose slowly, watching the nose carefully for the first indication of yaw that rudder cannot prevent, whereupon the nose is lowered and the power reduced on the operating engine as described above. Should this demonstration be mistakenly attempted with the engine feathered instead of windmilling, it might well be impossible to recover from an inadvertent spin without the use of power from the inside engine, which of course, would be unavailable if feathered.

C. Use of engine-out best rate of climb speed, and *D. Effects of airplane configuration on engine-out performance.* An applicant who has studied his manual and practiced the techniques required in this demonstration should have no difficulty with these sections.

E. Engine failure on takeoff. The criticism of feathering procedures in paragraph VI-A is especially valid here.

F. Engine-out approach and landing. Some applicants have become so absorbed in the landing that they have forgotten the "GUMP" check and attempted to land wheels up. This is not only embarrassing but disqualifying.

G. Emergency operations. An applicant who has studied his manual and knows his sytems should have no trouble with this section. However, it's worth mentioning to applicants with pressurized airplanes that an emergency descent simulation is required.

5.

Center-thrust twins

The center-thrust twin-engine airplane has both engines located down the center of the longitudinal axis of the airplane, one engine being located ahead of the aircraft cabin and the other aft. Among current production aircraft this configuration is best illustrated by the Cessna 336 Skymaster shown in the flight photo on the next page.

This arrangement means that the failure of one engine will not cause the airplane to yaw as it would in twins with the engines conventionally located in each wing, and thus some of the special problems in single-engine emergency procedure do not arise in the center-thrust twin.

In the conventional engine arrangement the pilot must know the two important airspeeds, VMC and single-engine best-rate-of-climb speed. Since the center-thrust twin does not yaw toward its dead engine, the pilot has no rudder control problem, but merely needs to know the stall speed with one engine out just as he would in a single-engine airplane.

The pilot of the center-thrust twin should know his single-engine best-rate-of-climb speed so as to obtain maximum performance from his airplane in a single-engine emergency.

As in conventional twins, the center-thrust pilot must be careful not to feather the wrong engine.. However, in the Cessna Skymaster loss of thrust of one engine is indicated by a small red light on the end of the prop control which is to be feathered, and the pilot feathers the prop which is lighted.

Following is the recommended procedure for engine-out emergencies in the Cessna 336 Skymaster:

Engine-out on takeoff (with sufficient runway remaining).
    (1) Cut power and decelerate to a stop. *Note:* The airplane can be accelerated from a standing start to 80 mph on the ground, and then decelerated to a stop with heavy braking within 1,900 feet of

Landing the Cessna 336 with front engine feathered. (*Cessna Aircraft Corp.*)

the starting point of the takeoff run at sea level, and within 2,400 feet of the starting point at 5,000 feet elevation. These distances are based on gross weight and no wind.

Engine-out after takeoff (without sufficient runway ahead).
(1) Throttles—full forward.
(2) Propellers—high rpm.
(3) Determine inoperative engine (from thrust warning light and engine rpm).
(4) Propeller—feather inoperative engine.
(5) Wing flaps—retract, in small increments, (if extended).
(6) Climb out at 90 mph.
(7) Cowl flaps (operative engine)—OPEN, as required.
(8) Secure inoperative engine as follows:
   a. Ignition switch—OFF.
   b. Alternator switch—OFF.
   c. Mixture—idle cut-off.
   d. Cowl flaps—CLOSED.
   e. Fuel Selector—FUEL OFF.

Engine-out during flight.
(1) Determine inoperative engine (check thrust warning lights).
(2) Power—increase as required.
(3) Mixture—adjust for altitude.

Before securing inoperative engine:
(1) Check fuel flow; if deficient, turn on auxiliary fuel pump. *Note:* If fuel selector valve handle is on AUXILIARY TANK, switch to MAIN TANK.
(2) Check fuel quantity and switch to opposite tank if necessary.
(3) Check ignition switches.

If proper corrective action was taken, engine will re-start. If it does not, secure it as follows:
  (1) Mixture—idle cut-off.
  (2) Propeller—FEATHER.
  (3) Turn off auxiliary fuel pump, alternator, and ignition switches and fuel selector valve.
  (4) Cowl flaps—CLOSED.

Single-engine approach.
  (1) Wing flaps—minimum setting necessary until landing is assured.
  (2) Airspeed—90 to 100 mph in approach.

Single-engine go-around.
  (1) Power—full throttle and 2800 rpm.
  (2) Airspeed—90 mph (80 mph with obstacles ahead).
  (3) Wing flaps—retract to 10 deg.
  (4) Cowl flaps—OPEN (on operating engine).
  (5) Wing flaps—retract after obstacles are cleared and a safe altitude and airspeed are reached.

Engine re-starts in flight after feathering practice.
  (1) Radio switches—OFF.
  (2) Fuel selector: front engine—LEFT MAIN.
  (2) Fuel selector: rear engine—RIGHT MAIN.
  (3) Throttle—advance (one inch).
  (4) Propeller—high rpm.
  (5) Auxiliary fuel pump switch—HIGH.
  (6) Mixture—adjust for a fuel flow between 2-6 gallons/hour.
  (7) Ignition switch—START (until engine starts windmilling).

  NOTE: With the operational propeller unfeathering system installed, the propeller will automatically windmill when the propeller pitch lever is moved to the high rpm position, at speeds above 110 mph.

PILOT RATINGS FOR MULTIENGINE AIRPLANES WITH ENGINES IN OR ON THE FUSELAGE

Flight Standards Service Release No. 467

Several new types of small multiengine airplanes are under development with engines so arranged that the failure of one does not require the application of multiengine pilot techniques. Among these are airplanes with jet engines in or on the fuselage, with multiple engines driving a common propeller shaft, and with engines arranged in tandem at either end of the fuselage.

We have received numerous inquiries on the pilot rating appropriate to these airplanes. They are in fact "multiengine" in that they have more than one engine, and our flight evaluation of one of them has indicated that the complexity of their operation is comparable with that of other current light twin-engine airplanes.

Accordingly, a pilot who conducts operations for which he is required by the regulations to hold an appropriate aircraft rating in such an airplane must possess a valid multiengine rating.

These airplanes do not present the directional and lateral control difficulties when an engine fails which are characteristic of multiengine airplanes with engines on the wings, and so cannot effectively train pilots to cope with engine-out emergencies involving minimum control speeds. Because of this, multiengine ratings issued to pilots tested in them will be appropriately limited: *Airplane multiengine land (or sea)—limited to center thrust.*

PILOT FLIGHT TEST
CESSNA MODEL 336 SKYMASTER

Flight Standards Service Release No. 473

The Cessna Aircraft Company, Wichita, Kansas, has suggested a number of flight test items for the conduct of emergency engine-out procedures in their Model 336 tandem-engine airplane. These items will be used by Inspectors and Pilot Examiners for the conduct of pilot certificate or rating tests in this airplane:

(1) Cut mixture on front engine and show rate of climb with windmilling propeller, compared to feathered propeller. (a) Illustrate effect of wing flaps on climb performance. (b) Demonstrate engine-out stalls (power on) in straight and turning flight.

(2) Repeat procedure with rear engine inoperative.

(3) Simulate an engine failure at approximately 1.1 times stalling speed (1.1 Vs$_1$) in takeoff configuration to show climb-out capabilities and engine-out procedures.

(4) Demonstrate loss of rpm associated with complete power loss at various speeds from stall to cruise (Vs to Vc).

(5) Demonstrate single-engine landing with inoperative engine idling at "zero thrust" rpm.

(6) Demonstrate in-flight unfeathering of propeller.

Ratings issued on the basis of flight tests in these airplanes will be appropriately limited *Airplane multiengine land - limited to center thrust.*

6.

Light twins: capsule data

In the following summaries of specifications and performance data on the most popular of the current light twins,
these abbreviations are used throughout:

  VMC: minimum control speed (single engine).
  SE BROC: single-engine best rate of climb speed.
  SE BAOC: single-engine best angle of climb speed.

PIPER APACHE

VMC . . . . 85 mph

SE BROC . . . . 95 mph

Fuel . . . . 80 oct. in 150 hp models, 100 oct. in 160 hp.

Fuel capacity . . . . Two 36 gal. main tanks, two optional 18 gal. aux. tanks, total 72 gals. without aux., 108 with aux.

Max. gear speed . . . . . 125 mph

Max. flap speed . . . . . 100 mph

Takeoff power setting . . Full throttle, 2700 rpm

Climb power setting . . . 25 in., 2400 rpm

Cruise power setting . . . 23 in., 2300 rpm, or 65% power from chart.

Engines . . . . Lycoming 0-320 (150 hp) and 0-320B (160 hp).

Gear & flap operation . . Hydraulic, with pump on left engine. Hand pump provides for pressure manually. Gear takes 30-40 strokes to pump down, flaps 12.

Emergency gear extend . . If unable to pump down, a CO_2 bottle can be used to supply pressure. Control is beneath cover plate under pilot seat.

Fuel consumption . . . . . 16.3 gph at 65% power.

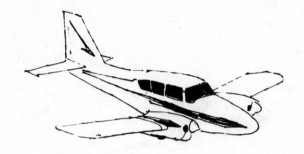

PIPER AZTEC

VMC . . . . 80 mph
SE BROC . . . . 110 mph
Fuel . . . . 100 octane.
Fuel capacity . . . . Four 36 gallon tanks, total 144.
Max. gear speed . . . . . 150 mph
Max. flap speed . . . . . 125 mph
Takeoff power setting . . Full throttle, 2575 rpm
Climb power setting . . . 24 in., 2400 rpm
Cruise power setting . . . 23 in., 2300 rpm, or 65% power from chart.
Engines . . . . Lycoming 0-540-A1B5, 250 hp.
Gear & flap operation . . Same as Apache.
Emergency gear extend . . Same as Apache.
Fuel consumption . . . . . 24 gph at 65% power.

BEECH D-18

VMC	95 mph
SE BROC	111 mph
Fuel	80 octane
Fuel capacity	Two main tanks 76 gals. each, two aux. tanks 25 gals. each, optional nose tank 80 gals.
Max. gear speed	125 mph
Max. flap speed	120 mph
Takeoff power setting . .	36.5 in., 2300 rpm.
Climb power setting . . .	30 in., 2000 rpm.
Cruise power setting . . .	27 in., 1900 rpm, or 65% power from chart.
Engines	Pratt & Whitney Wasp Jr., 450 hp.
Gear & flap operation . .	Electric.
Emergency gear extend . .	Gear switch off, engage clutch on floor, pull handcrank out to crank down gear.
Fuel consumption	50 gph @ 65% power.

BEECH 65 QUEEN AIR

VMC	95 mph
SE BROC	117 mph
SE BAOC	104 mph
Fuel	100/130 octane
Fuel capacity	Two 44 gal. main tanks, four 23 gal. aux. tanks, std. 180 gals.; with two optional 25 gal. aux. tanks, 230 gals.
Max. gear speed	150 mph
Max. flap speed	150 mph
Takeoff power setting . .	45 in., 3200 rpm
Climb power setting . . .	40 in., 3000 rpm
Cruise power setting . . .	32 in., 2600 rpm, or 65% power from chart.
Engines	Lycoming IGSO-480, 340 hp
Gear & flap operation . .	Electric
Emergency gear extend . .	Pull circuit breaker, gear switch *down*, turn clutch lever clockwise to lock, remove land. gear extension handle and pump 50 strokes.
Fuel consumption	38 gph @ 65% power.

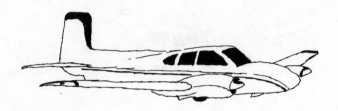

BEECH B-50 TWIN BONANZA

VMC	90 mph
SE BROC	100 mph
Fuel	100 oct.
Fuel capacity	Two 44 gal. main tanks, two 23 gal. aux. tanks, total 134 gallons.
Max. gear speed	125 mph
Max. flap speed	125 mph
Takeoff power setting	Full throttle, 3400 rpm
Climb power setting	Full throttle, 3100 rpm
Cruise power setting	22 in., 2650 rpm, or 65% power from chart. Mixture control automatic, do not lean.
Engines	Lycoming G0-480, 360 hp.
Gear & flap operation	Electric.
Emergency gear extend	Clutch and extension lever beneath co-pilot seat. Move clutch to right, and stroke ratchet about 150 times.
Fuel consumption	26 gph at 65% power.

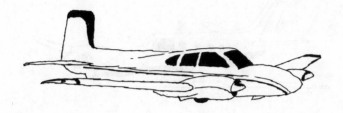

BEECH D-50 TWIN BONANZA

VMC	90 mph
SE BROC	110 mph
Fuel	100 oct.
Fuel capacity	Two 44 gal. main tanks, two 23 gal. aux. tanks, total 134 gals; or two additional 23 gal. aux. tanks, total 180.
Max. gear speed	150 mph
Max. flap speed	135 mph
Takeoff power setting . .	Full throttle, 3400 rpm
Climb power setting . . .	Full throttle, 3100 rpm
Cruise power setting . . .	22 in., 2650 rpm, or 65% power from chart, mixture control automatic, do not lean.
Engines	Lycoming GO-480-C2C6, 295 hp.
Gear & flap operation . .	Electric.
Emergency gear extend . .	Same as Beech B-50.
Fuel consumption	32.5 gph @ 65% power.

BEECH DUKE

VMC . . . . 85 kts.

SE BROC . . . . 110 kts.

SE BAOC . . . . 100 kts.

Fuel . . . . 100/130 octane

Fuel capacity . . . . . . Std. 142 gals., optional 178 or 204 gals.

Max. gear speed . . . . . 175 kts.

Max. flap speed . . . . . 175 kts. for 15°, 135 kts. for 15-30°.

Takeoff power setting . . 41 in., 2900 rpm.

Climb power setting . . . 35.5 in., 2750 rpm.

Cruise power setting . . . 28.2., 2650 rpm for 65% power.

Engines . . . . Lycoming TIO-541-E1A4, 380 hp.

Gear & flap operation . . Electric

Emergency gear extend . . Gear switch down, pull gear circuit breaker, handcrank under left front seat, crank 50 turns, disengage crank.

Fuel consumption . . . . . 36.6 gph @ 65% power.

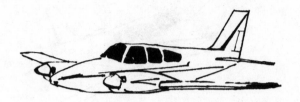

BEECH 55 BARON

VMC . . . . 92 mph
SE BROC . . . . 115 mph
SE BAOC . . . . 103 mph
Fuel . . . . 100 oct.
Fuel capacity . . . . . . Two 25 gal. main tanks, two 31 gal. aux. tanks, total 112 gals.; or two optional main tanks of 39 gals. each, total 140 gallons.
Max. gear speed . . . . . 150 mph
Max. flap speed . . . . . 130 mph
Takeoff power setting . . Full throttle, 2700 rpm
Climb power setting . . . 25 in., 2500 rpm
Cruise power setting . . . 23 in., 2300 rpm, or 65% power from chart.
Engines . . . . Continental 10-470-L, 260 hp.
Gear & flap operation . . Electric.
Emergency gear extend . . Handcrank located behind front seats.
Fuel consumption . . . . . 26.5 gph @ 65% power.

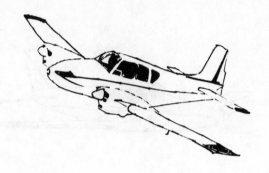

BEECH 95 TRAVELAIR

VMC	84 mph
SE BROC	100 mph
Fuel	100 oct.
Fuel capacity	Two 25 gal. main tanks, two 17 gal. aux. tanks, total 84 gals.; or two optional aux. tanks of 31 gals. each, total 112 gals.
Max. gear speed	150 mph
Max. flap speed	130 mph
Takeoff power setting . .	Full throttle, 2700 rpm
Climb power setting . . .	25 in., 2500 rpm
Cruise power setting . . .	23 in., 2350 rpm
Engines	Lycoming 0-360-A1A, 180 hp.
Gear & flap operation . .	Electric.
Emergency gear extend . .	Handcrank located behind front seats.
Fuel consumption	17.6 gph @ 65% power.

CESSNA 310

VMC	93 mph
SE BROC	121 mph
SE BAOC	110 mph
Fuel	100 oct.
Fuel capacity	Two 50 gal. main tanks, in each wing tip
Max. gear speed	130 mph
Max. flap speed	130 mph
Takeoff power setting . .	Full throttle, 2600 rpm
Climb power setting . . .	25 in., 2400 rpm.
Cruise power setting . . .	23 in., 2300 rpm, or 65% from power chart.
Engines	Continental 0-740B, 240 hp.
Gear & flap operation . .	Electric.
Emergency gear extend . .	Handcrank beside pilot seat, 60 turns.
Fuel consumption	25.4 gph @ 65% power.

CESSNA 401-402

VMC	95 in air, 105 for takeoff
SE BROC	118 mph
SE BAOC	114 mph
Fuel	100/130 octane
Fuel capacity	Two 50 gal. main tanks, two opt. 20 gal. aux. tanks, total 140 gals.
Max. gear speed	160 mph
Max. flap speed	180 mph for 15°, 160 for 15-45°.
Takeoff power setting	34.5 in., 2700 rpm
Climb power setting	29.5 in., 2450 rpm
Cruise power setting	29.0 in., 2300 rpm, or 65% power from chart.
Engines	Continental TSIO-520-E, 300 hp
Gear & flap operation	Electric
Emergency gear extend	Pull circuit breaker, gear switch *neutral*, handcrank under left front seat, crank 54 turns.
Fuel consumption	28.5 gph @ 65% power.

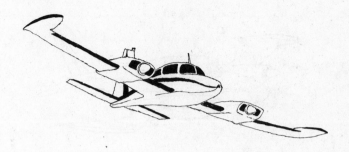

CESSNA 310-G

VMC . . . . 95 mph
SE BROC . . . . 117 mph
SE BAOC . . . . 105 mph
Fuel . . . . 100 oct.
Fuel capacity . . . . Two 50 gal. main tanks, two optional 15 gal.
aux. tanks.
Max. gear speed 140
Max. flap speed . . . . . 160 for 15 deg., 140 for 15-45 deg.
Takeoff power setting . . Full throttle, 2625 rpm.
Climb power setting . . . 24 in., 2450 rpm.
Cruise power setting . . . 23 in., 2300 rpm.
Engines . . . . Continental TSIO-470-B, 260 hp.
Gear & flap operation . . Electric.
Emergency gear extend . . Same as 310.
Fuel consumption . . . . . 24.5 gph @ 65% power.

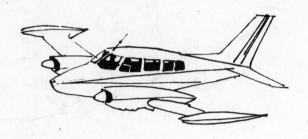

CESSNA 320 SKYNIGHT

VMC . . . . 95 mph
SE BROC . . . . 117 mph
SE BAOC . . . . 105 mph
Fuel . . . . 100 oct.
Fuel capacity . . . . Two 50 gal. main tanks and two optional 15 gal. aux. tanks.
Max. gear speed . . . . . 140 mph
Max. flap speed . . . . . 160 for 15 deg. 140 for 15-45 deg.
Takeoff power setting . . Full throttle 35 in., 2600 rpm.
Climb power setting . . . 29 in., 2450 rpm.
Cruise power setting . . . 28 in., 2300 rpm, or 65% power from chart.
Engines . . . . Continental TSIO-470-B, 260 hp.
Gear & flap operation . . Electric.
Emergency gear extend . . Same as 310.
Fuel consumption . . . . . 24.4 gph @ 65% power.

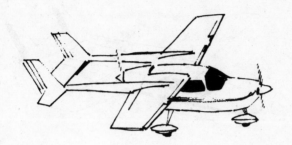

CESSNA SKYMASTER

SE BROC . . . . 90 mph
Fuel . . . . 100 oct.
Fuel capacity . . . . . . Main tanks 92 gals., optional aux. tanks of 38 gals.
Takeoff power setting . . Full throttle, 2800 rpm.
Climb power setting . . . 25 in., 2500 rpm.
Cruise power setting . . . 23 in., 2300 rpm., or 65% power from chart.
Engines . . . . Continental I0-360-A, 210 hp.
Gear & flap operation . . Gear fixed, flaps electric.
Fuel consumption . . . . . 18.5 gph @ 65% power.

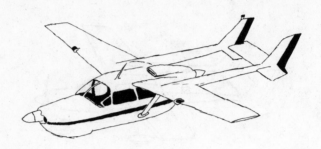

CESSNA SUPER SKYMASTER
(Retractable Gear)

SE BROC . . . . 99 mph
SE BAOC . . . . 89 mph
Fuel . . . . 100 oct.
Fuel capacity . . . . Main tanks 92 gals., optional aux. tanks of
                            38 gals.
Max. gear speed . . . . . 140 mph
Max. flap speed . . . . . . 160 mph for 1/3, 120 mph for over 1/3.
Takeoff power setting . . . Full throttle, 2800 rpm.
Climb power setting . . . 24 in., 2600 rpm.
Cruise power setting . . . 23 in., 2300 rpm, or 65% power from chart.
Engines . . . . Continental IO-360-C/D
Gear and flap operation . Hydraulic, pump on front engine.
Emergency gear extend . . Pump down with emergency hand pump.
Fuel consumption . . . . . 19.9 gph @ 65% power.

CESSNA 411

VMC . . . . 105 mph
SE BROC . . . . 120 mph
SE BAOC . . . . 115 mph
Fuel . . . . 100 oct.
Fuel capacity . . . . Two 50 gal. main tanks, two 35 gal. aux. tanks, and two optional 13 gal. additional aux. tanks.
Max. gear speed . . . . . 160 mph
Max. flap speed . . . . . . 180 mph for 15 deg. and 160 mph for 15-45 deg.
Takeoff power setting . . . Full throttle, 2400 rpm.
Climb power setting . . . 29 in., 2100 rpm.
Cruise power setting . . . 29 in., 2100 rpm for max. cruise (75%) or consult power computer.
Engines . . . . Continental GTSIO-520-C.
Gear and flap operation . Electric.
Emergency gear extend . . Handcrank below right front edge of pilot seat; pull circuit breaker, gear switch neutral, crank clockwise approx. 58 turns.
Fuel consumption . . . . . 37.2 gal. @ 75%, 32 gal. @ 65% power.

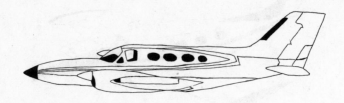

CESSNA 421, 421A

VMC . . . . 107 mph in air, 120 for takeoff.
SE BROC . . . . 120 mph
SE BAOC . . . . 120 mph
Fuel . . . . 100/130 octane
Fuel capacity . . . . Two 50 gal. main tanks, two 35 gal. aux.
tanks, std. fuel 170 gals.; two 13 gal. outboard
aux. tanks optional; two 26 gal. wing locker
tanks optional.
Max. gear speed . . . . . 165 mph
Max. flap speed . . . . . 180 mph for 15°, 165 for 30-45°.
Takeoff power setting . . 39.5 in., 2275 rpm.
Climb power setting . . . 32.5 in., 1950 rpm.
Cruise power setting . . . 32.5 in., 1950 rpm for 75% power, or
31.0 in., 1800 rpm for 65% power.
Engines . . . . Continental GTSIO-520-D, 375 hp.
Gear & flap operation . . Electric
Emergency gear extend . . Same as 411, but 54 turns.
Fuel consumption . . . . . 41.3 gph for 75% power, 36.3 for 65%.

CESSNA 310-Q

VMC . . . . : . . .	86 mph in air, 105 for takeoff
SE BROC	116 mph
SE BAOC	108 mph
Fuel	100/130 octane
Fuel Capacity	Two 50 gal. main tanks, two optional 20 gal. aux. tanks, 140 gals. total (1,080 lbs.)
Max. gear speed	160 mph
Max. flap speed	180 for 15°, 160 for 15-35°
Takeoff power setting . . .	Full throttle, 2625 rpm
Climb power setting	24 in., 2450 rpm
Cruise power setting	22 in., 2300 rpm, or 65% power from chart or computer
Engines	Continental 10-470-VO, 260 hp
Gear & flap operation . .	Electric
Emergency gear extend . .	Handcrank below right front edge of pilot seat; pull circuit breaker, gear switch neutral, crank clockwise approx. 52 turns.
Fuel consumption	24.3 gph @ 65% power (146 lbs. per hr.)

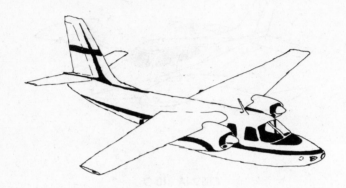

AERO COMMANDER 560E

VMC . . . . 80 mph
SE BROC . . . . 95-105 mph
Fuel . . . . 100 oct.
Fuel capacity . . . . 156 gal. center tank, two 33.5 aux. tanks,
total 223 gals.
Max. gear speed . . . . . 160 mph
Max. flap speed . . . . . 130 full flap, 150 for ½.
Takeoff power setting . . Full throttle, 3400 rpm.
Climb power setting . . . Full throttle, 3000 rpm.
Cruise power setting . . . 22 in., 2650 rpm, or 65% power from chart.
Engines . . . . Lycoming GO-480, 295 hp.
Gear & flap operation . . Hydraulic, pump on left engine.
Fuel consumption . . . . . 27 gph @ 65% power.

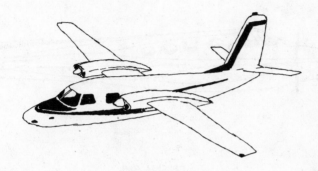

AERO COMMANDER 680F

VMC . . . . 100 mph
SE BAOC . . . . 110 mph
Fuel . . . . 100 oct.
Fuel capacity . . . . . . 223 gallons.
Max. gear speed . . . . . 180 mph
Max. flap speed . . . . . 150 mph
Takeoff power setting . . 47 in., 3400 rpm.
1st power reduction . . . . 45 in., 3200 rpm.
Secondary climb power . . 40 in., 3000 rpm.
Cruise power setting . . . 32 in., 2600 rpm, or 65% power from chart.
Gear & flap operation . . Hydraulic, pump on both engines.
Engines . . . . Lycoming IGSO-540-B1A, 380 hp.
Fuel consumption . . . . . 45.2 gph @ 65% power.

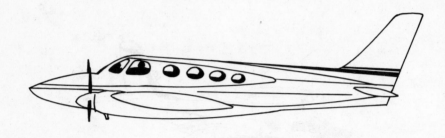

CESSNA 340

VMC . . . . 97 mph in air, 105 for takeoff
SE BROC . . . . 115 mph
SE BAOC . . . . 110 mph
Fuel . . . . 100/130 octane
Fuel Capacity . . . . . . Two 50 gal. main tanks, two optional 20 gal. aux. tanks, 140 gals. total (1,080 lbs.)
Max. gear speed . . . . . 160 mph
Max. flap speed . . . . . . 180 for 15°, 160 for 15-45°
Takeoff power setting . . . 33 in., 2700 rpm
Climb power setting . . . . 28 in., 2450 rpm
Cruise power setting . . . . 27 in., 2300 rpm, or 64% power from chart or computer
Engines . . . . Continental TSIO-520-K, 285 hp
Gear & flap operation . . Electric
Emergency gear extend . . Handcrank below right front edge of pilot seat; pull circuit breaker, gear switch neutral, crank clockwise approx. 54 turns.
Fuel consumption . . . . . 28.3 gph @ 64% power (169.8 lbs. per hr.)

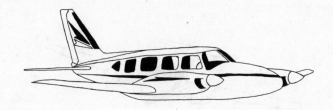

PIPER NAVAJO

VMC	85 mph
SE BROC	110 mph
SE BAOC	106 mph
Fuel	100/130 octane
Fuel capacity	Two 56 gal. inboard tanks, two 40 gal. outboard tanks, total 192 gals.
Max. gear speed	150 mph
Max. flap speed	150 mph
Takeoff power setting . .	38 in., 2575 rpm
Climb power setting . . .	35 in., 2400 rpm
Cruise power setting . . .	28 in., 2400 rpm, or 65% power from chart.
Engines	Lycoming TIO-540-A, 310 hp.
Gear & flap operation . .	Gear hydraulic, pumps on both engines; flaps electric.
Emergency gear extend . .	Hand pump on floor between pilot seats, gear selector *down*, pump 60 strokes.
Fuel consumption	27.8 gph @ 65% power.

TWIN COMANCHE, PA-30

VMC . . . . 80 mph
SE BROC . . . . 105 mph
Fuel . . . . 100 oct.
Fuel capacity . . . . Two 27 gallon main tanks, two 15 gal. aux.,
total capacity 84 gals.
Max. gear speed . . . . . 150 mph
Max. flap speed . . . . . 125 mph
Takeoff power setting . . Full throttle.
Climb power setting . . . 24 in., 2400 rpm.
Cruise power setting . . . 22 in., 2300 rpm, or 65% power from chart.
Engines . . . . Lycoming 10-320B, 160 hp.
Gear & flap operation . . Electric.
Emergency gear extend . . Emergency system beneath front floorboards.
Fuel consumption . . . . . 15.5 gph, @ 65% power.

AEROSTAR 600

VMC	97 mph
SE BROC	130 mph
SE BAOC	120 mph
Fuel	100/130 octane
Fuel capacity	174.5 gals.
Max. gear speed	180 mph
Max. flap speed	180 mph for 20°, 150 for 20-45°.
Takeoff power setting . .	Full throttle, 2575 rpm.
Climb power setting . . .	Full throttle, 2575 rpm (max. continuous)
Cruise power setting . . .	22 in., 2300 rpm, or 65% power from chart.
Engines	Lycoming IO-540-G1B5, 290 hp.
Gear & flap operation . .	Hydraulic, pump on right engine.
Emergency gear extend . .	Gear handle down, after gear free-falls to locked, cycle gear handle *up* then *down* for lock to be fully effective.
Fuel consumption	30 gph @ 65% power.

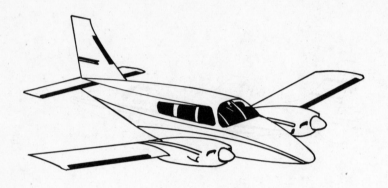

PIPER SENECA, PA-34

VMC	80 mph in air, 100 for takeoff
SE BROC	105 mph
Fuel	100/130 octane
Fuel Capacity	Two 47.5 gal. mains, 95 gals. total
Max. gear speed	150 mph
Max. flap speed	160 mph for 10°, 140-25°, 125-40°
Takeoff power setting	Full throttle, 2700 rpm
Climb power setting	25 in., 2500 rpm
Cruise power setting	21 in., 2400 rpm, or 65% power from tables
Engines	Lycoming IO-360-C1E6 (left engine) Lycoming LIO-360-C1E6 (right engine)
Gear & flap operation	Gear hydraulic (electric pump); flaps manual
Emergency gear extend	AS 100 mph, gear switch DOWN, pull gear extension knob.
Fuel consumption	18.3 gph @ 65% power

7.

Larger multiengine aircraft
(*type rating*)

The Federal Aviation Regulations prohibit a pilot from serving as pilot-in-command of an aircraft exceeding 12,500 pounds maximum certified weight when carrying passengers or operated for hire unless, in addition to proper category and class ratings, he also holds an appropriate *type* rating. A list of the type ratings issued by the Federal Aviation Agency is provided at the end of this chapter.

An applicant for a multiengine type rating is given the flight test prescribed in AC 61-57, the FAA *Flight Test Guide,* and reprinted in this chapter.

In reference to transport category aircraft, certain standard terms are used differently; pilots should be familiar with the distinction. For example, the light-twin pilot thinks of Vmc and SE best rate of climb speed, whereas the pilot of transport category type aircraft uses the two speeds known as V1 and V2. These are explained in the following definitions:

V1—The critical-engine failure speed.

V2—The takeoff safety speed.

Critical engine—That engine the failure of which gives the most adverse effect on the airplane flight characteristics.

VSO—The stalling speed with wing flaps in the landing position.

VS1—The stalling speed with wing flaps in the takeoff position.

VMC—The minimum control speed with the critical engine inoperative and the operating engine at full takeoff power, wing flaps and cowl flaps in takeoff position, propeller windmilling on critical engine unless equipped with automatic feathering.

VFE—The maximum speed with wing flaps extended.

VLE—The maximum speed at which the airplane can be flown safely with the landing gear extended.

Accelerate-stop distance—the sum of the distance required to accelerate the airplane from a standing start to the speed V1, plus the distance required to bring the airplane to a full stop should the critical engine fail at speed V1.

In the execution of a *T* category takeoff the pilot would cut the throttles and stop the airplane should an engine fail below V1; below this speed the airplane can be stopped in the remaining runway distance. Above speed V1 the airplane can be accelerated to safe takeoff speed V2 and complete the takeoff at this speed, clearing obstacles with a margin of safety.

The airplane is held on the ground during takeoff run until V2 is reached. This is most important in the event of an engine failure between V1 and V2. Takeoff is made at V2, the gear being raised as soon as the airplane is definitely off the ground. In an emergency engine-out takeoff, the speed is held at the safety speed V2, and the flaps are held at takeoff settings until all obstacles are cleared.

The takeoff safety speed V2 shall be at least 1.2 times VS1 for twin-engine airplanes, and 1.1 times the minimum

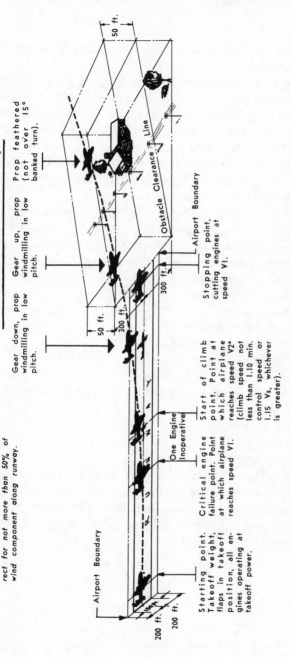

Note: Correct for elevation of airport and runway gradient. Correct for not more than 50% of wind component along runway.

One-Engine-Out Climb At Takeoff Weight

Gear down, prop windmilling in low pitch.

Gear up, prop windmilling in low pitch.

Prop feathered (not over 15° banked turn).

Obstacle Clearance Line

Airport Boundary

Stopping point, cutting engines at speed VI.

Start of climb point. Point at which airplane reaches speed V2* (climb speed not less than 1.10 min. control speed or 1.15 Vs, whichever is greater).

Critical engine failure point. Point at which airplane reaches speed VI.

One Engine Inoperative

Starting point. Takeoff weight, flaps in takeoff position, all engines operating at takeoff power.

Airport Boundary

200 ft.

200 ft.

50 ft.

300 ft.

50 ft.

300 ft.

50 ft.

THE AIRPLANE SHALL BE RUN UP TO A SPECIFIED SPEED AND FROM THERE BE ABLE TO:

1. Stop within the airport boundaries.
2. Continue with one engine inoperative and clear obstacles as shown.

* 1.2Vs, for airplanes with two engines.
  1.15Vs, for airplanes with more than two engines. } Vs, = Stall speed with takeoff configuration.

Fig. 11—T-category takeoff.

control speed VMC.

See Fig. 11 for illustration of V1 and V2 in a Transport-Category takeoff.

It is even more important for the pilot of a Transport Category airplane to study the Airplane Flight Manual thoroughly. This is borne out by the fact that the airlines send their new co-pilots to ground school for several weeks of study on the airplane and its systems.

The larger airplane will be more complex, and the pilot who studies the Airplane Flight Manual will become acquainted with the following topics:

Calculating takeoff weight limitations from charts.

Determining critical engine failure speed from charts.

Determining takeoff flap settings for various altitudes.

Determining landing weight limitations from charts.

Calculating weight and balance.

Determining stall speeds from charts.

Flap management

Powerplant management

Supercharger management.

Mixture control management.

Augmentors and their function.

Propeller management, including reversal and auto-feathering.

Anti-icing systems.

Pressurization.

Emergency procedures.

It is not within the scope of this book to attempt to go into detail on each of the above items inasmuch as they vary with individual airplanes, but they are listed here simply to emphasize the need for the pilot's study of the airplane manual.

TYPE RATING FLIGHT TEST

(The following material is reprinted from Section 2, Type Rating, *Flight Test Guide, Multiengine Airplane Class and Type Ratings, FAA Publication AC 61-57*).

I. PREFLIGHT OPERATIONS

Objective. To determine that the applicant has a practical knowledge of the airplane, its operation and limitations.

A. Equipment check (oral and written)

1. Description. The applicant may be asked to present and explain the airplane documents to be carried on board. He may be asked to demonstrate a practical knowledge of: (1) the airplane, its powerplants, systems, and components, and their operation; (2) normal, abnormal, and emergency procedures and the operations and limitations related thereto; (3) flight planning procedures using the manufacturer's published recommendations to determine such operational factors as required runway lengths, critical performance speeds, fuel requirements, and weight and balance limitations.

2. Acceptable performance guidelines. The applicant's performance shall be evaluated on the basis of his knowledge of the airplane, its systems and components, and his ability to make a practical application of performance data and limitations contained in the manufacturer's published recommendations.

B. Inspection

1. Description. The applicant may be asked to conduct a visual inspection of the interior and exterior of the airplane, explaining the purpose for inspecting each item. He should demonstrate the use of the prestart checklist, appropriate control system checks, starting procedures, and radio and equipment checks prior to flight.

2. Acceptable performance guidelines. The applicant's performance shall be evaluated on the accuracy of his explanation of the purpose for inspecting each item and the thoroughness of his inspection.

C. Taxiing

1. Description. The applicant may be asked to demonstrate taxiing, sailing, or docking procedures in compliance with instructions issued by the appropriate traffic control authority or by the examiner.

  2. Acceptable performance guidelines. Evaluation shall be made on the basis of the applicant's attention to safety; proficiency in handling the aircraft; consideration for other aircraft and personnel on ramps and taxiways; the use of power, brakes, and flight controls for directional control; and the proper use of nosewheel steering, tailwheel lock, or water rudder as applicable.

D. Powerplant checks

  1. Description. The applicant may be asked to make the necessary checks to assure the airplane's immediate readiness for flight.

  2. Acceptable performance guidelines. The applicant shall be evaluated on the proficiency and thoroughness with which the powerplant checks are accomplished and the thoroughness of the knowledge displayed of the airplane engines, systems, and related operational checks.

II. TAKEOFFS

  Objective. To determine that the applicant is competent in performing takeoffs under normal and emergency conditions and under various meteorological conditions.

A. Normal takeoffs

  1. Description. The applicant may be asked to perform one normal takeoff which, for the purposes of this operation, begins when the airplane is taxied into position on the runway to be used.

  2. Acceptable performance guidelines. Performance shall be evaluated on the basis of the applicant's takeoff technique, judgment, observance of traffic patterns and control tower instructions, coordination, and smoothness. Airplane configuration, airspeed, and operational procedures shall be in accordance with those recommended in the applicable operating instructions for the airplane being used.

B. Crosswind takeoff

  1. Description. The applicant may be asked to perform one crosswind takeoff, if safe and practicable under the existing conditions.

2. Acceptable performance guidelines. Performance shall be evaluated on the basis of the applicant's takeoff technique, judgment, observance of traffic patterns and control tower instructions, coordination, and smoothness. Airplane configuration, airspeed, and operational procedures shall be in accordance with those recommended in the applicable operating instructions for the airplane being used.

C. Powerplant failure

1. Description. The applicant may be asked to perform one takeoff with a simulated failure of the most critical powerplant at a speed determined to be appropriate for the category (transport or nontransport) and type airplane used for the check.

2. Acceptable performance guidelines. Performance shall be evaluated on the basis of the applicant's takeoff technique, judgment, observance of traffic patterns and control tower instructions, coordination, and smoothness. Airplane configuration, airspeed, and operational procedures shall be in accordance with those recommended in the applicable operating instructions for the airplane being used.

D. Instrument takeoff

The applicant for a multiengine airplane type rating who does *not* hold or is *not* concurrently obtaining an instrument rating (airplane) may be asked to show competency only in those instrument maneuvers listed in Chapt. 4, class rating, of this manual.

1. Description. The applicant may be asked to perform one takeoff with instrument conditions simulated after reaching an altitude of 100 feet above the runway elevation.

2. Acceptable performance guidelines. Performance shall be evaluated on the basis of the applicant's takeoff technique, judgment, adherence to control tower instructions, coordination, and smoothness. Airplane configuration, airspeed, and operational procedures shall be in accordance with those recommended in the applicable operating instructions for the airplane being used.

III. INSTRUMENT PROCEDURES

Objective. To determine that the applicant can adhere to

actual or simulated ATC clearances, including assigned radials and proper use of navigation facilities.

A. Area departures and arrivals
   1. Description. The applicant may be asked to perform area departure and arrival procedures, demonstrating the proper response to actual or simulated ATC instructions and the proper use of navigation facilities.
   2. Acceptable performance guidelines. Evaluation shall be made on the basis of the applicant's acceptance and adherence to instructions and his knowledge of, and use of, available navigation facilities; also his knowledge of, and observance of, airspeed limits relative to altitude and distance from the airport.

B. Holding
   1. Description. The applicant may be asked to demonstrate entering, maintaining, and leaving holding patterns. This procedure may be performed in connection with area departures or arrivals.
   2. Acceptable performance guidelines. Evaluation shall be made on the basis of the applicant's compliance with the holding direction/radial, timing, and staying within the holding airspace. The applicant shall maintain altitude within plus or minus 100 feet of the assigned altitude. Holding airspeed shall be maintained within plus or minus 10 knots of that airspeed recommended for holding in the airplane being used.

C. Precision and nonprecision approaches
   1. Description. The applicant may be asked to perform one each of the following: (a) a normal ILS approach; (b) a nonprecision approach (ADF/VOR); and (c) an approach with simulated failure of one powerplant, by means of (a) or (b). Each approach (straight-in or circling) should be performed according to procedures approved for the facility used. For the purpose of these procedures, the approach begins when the airplane is over the initial fix for the procedure used or, as is frequently the case with vectoring by ATC, when cleared for the approach. In the case of a PAR procedure, the approach begins when handed-off to the final approach controller. The approach ends when the airplane touches the runway or when transition to a missed approach is complete.

2. Acceptable performance guidelines. Airplane configuration and airspeeds shall be in accordance with those recommended in the applicable operating instructions for the airplane being used. Arrival at the authorized minimum in position for a straight-in landing is an acceptable performance for nonprecision instrument approaches. The ILS approach, to be considered acceptable, shall be conducted so that glide slope and localizer indications do not exceed one dot deviation. Altitude shall be maintained within plus or minus 100 feet of prescribed altitude during initial approach, and within −0 to +50 feet of minimum descent altitude or decision height. Airspeed shall be controlled within plus or minus 10 knots of the recommended airspeed for the airplane configuration from the initial approach fix to the fix inbound and within −0 to +10 knots of reference airspeed with appropriate wind/gust factor adjustment from the final fix to the minimum descent altitude or decision height.

D. Missed approach

1. Description. The applicant may be asked to perform at least one complete missed approach procedure with simulated failure of one powerplant. The simulated powerplant failure may be given either before or after the missed approach procedure is initiated. This procedure may be performed independently or in conjunction with the approaches described under paragraphs C 1 (a) and (b) of this pilot operation. (Simulated powerplant failure should not be continued after the clean-up procedure has been performed.)

2. Acceptable performance guidelines. Evaluation shall be made on the basis of the applicant's judgment in deciding when to execute the missed approach, the appropriateness of his communications and navigation procedures, his ability to maintain positive airplane control and to operate all airplane systems in accordance with applicable operating instructions for the airplane being used. Descent below the MDA or DH, as appropriate, prior to initiation of the missed approach procedure shall be disqualifying except in those instances where the runway environment was in sight at MDA or DH.

IV. INFLIGHT MANEUVERS

Objective. To determine that the applicant is competent in controlling an airplane in a steep bank under maneuvering load factors while maintaining altitude and orientation; and, that he can recognize stalls in various airplane configurations and can make prompt and effective recoveries while in simulated instrument flight conditions. *Note:* The applicant for a multiengine type rating who does *not* hold or is *not* concurrently obtaining an instrument rating (airplane) may perform steep turns and stalls by visual references.

A. Steep turns

1. Description. The applicant may be asked to demonstrate at least one steep turn in each direction. Each steep turn should involve a bank angle of 45° with a heading change of 360°.

2. Acceptable performance guidelines. The applicant shall maintain altitude within plus or minus 100 feet of the entry altitude, and a bank angle of 45°, plus or minus 5°, after the turn is established, and recover within plus or minus 10° of the assigned headings. Airspeed shall be controlled within plus or minus 10 knots of that recommended for the airplane being used. Special attention shall be given to the applicant's smoothness, coordination, and orientation.

B. Stalls

1. Description. The applicant may be asked to demonstrate stalls. For the purpose of this maneuver, the stall is reached when there is a perceptible buffet or other response to initial stall entry. A stall demonstration may be required in each of the following flight configurations: (a) takeoff configuration (except in airplanes requiring zero flaps for takeoff); (b) clean configuration; and (c) landing configuration. At least one of these maneuvers should be performed using a bank angle between 15° and 30°.

2. Acceptable performance guidelines. The applicant shall recognize the approach to a stall when there is a perceptible buffet or from activation of stall warning devices. Recoveries shall be initiated at the first indication of a stall. The recoveries shall be accomplished positively and smoothly, using appropriate and coordinated flight and power controls and with the least loss of altitude consistent with the recovery of full control effectiveness. After recovery, the applicant shall make an expeditious return to the original altitude. Additional evaluation shall be made on the basis of the applicant's prompt, smooth, and positive control application.

V. APPROACHES AND LANDINGS

Objective. To determine that the applicant is competent in performing landings under normal, abnormal, and emergency conditions, and can safely reject a landing when required.

A. Normal landing

1. Description. The applicant may be asked to perform a normal approach and landing. For the purpose of this demonstration, the maneuver begins when the airplane enters the traffic pattern or begins an instrument approach and is completed at the end of the after-landing roll.

2. Acceptable performance guidelines. Traffic pattern airspeeds shall be controlled within −0 to +10 knots of that recommended for that type airplane and the appropriate airplane configuration until reaching final approach. Airspeed on the final approach shall be controlled with −0 to +10 knots of reference speed with appropriate wind/gust factor adjustment as recommended by the operating instructions for the airplane being used. Threshold airspeeds, also, shall be as recommended by those instructions with appropriate wind/gust factor adjustments.

B. Landing in sequence from an ILS approach

1. Description. The applicant may be asked to demonstrate a landing in sequence from an ILS approach, except that, if circumstances beyond his control prevent an actual landing, the examiner may accept an approach to a point where in his judgment a landing to a full stop could have been safely made.

2. Acceptable performance guidelines. Traffic pattern airspeeds shall be controlled within plus or minus 5 knots of the airspeed recommended by the operating instructions for the type airplane being used and the appropriate airplane configuration until reaching final approach. Airspeed on the final approach shall be controlled within −0 to +10 knots of reference speed with appropriate wind/gust factor adjustment as recommended by the operating instructions for the airplane being used. Threshold airspeeds, also, shall be as recommended by those instructions with appropriate wind/gust factor adjustments.

C. Crosswind landing

1. *Description.* The applicant may be asked to perform a crosswind landing, if considered safe and practical under existing conditions by examiner.

2. *Acceptable performance guidelines.* Traffic pattern airspeeds shall be controlled within plus or minus 5 knots of that recommended for the type airplane being used and the appropriate airplane configuration until reaching final approach. Airspeed on the final approach shall be controlled within −0 to +10 knots of reference speed with appropriate wind/gust factor adjustment as recommended by the operating instructions for the airplane being used. Threshold airspeeds, also, shall be as recommended by those instructions with appropriate wind/gust factor adjustments.

D. Engine-out landing

1. *Description.* The applicant may be asked to perform one approach to a landing with the simulated failure of 50% of the available powerplants (failed powerplants on one side). In the case of three-engine airplanes, an approved procedure which simulates the failure of two engines should be used (center and one outboard).

2. *Acceptable performance guidelines.* Traffic pattern airspeeds shall be controlled within plus or minus 6 knots of that recommended for the type airplane being used and the appropriate airplane configuration until reaching final approach. Airspeed on the final approach shall be controlled within −0 to +10 knots of reference speed with appropriate wind/gust factor adjustment as recommended by the operating instructions for the airplane being used. Threshold airspeeds, also, shall be as recommended by those instructions with appropriate wind/gust factor adjustments.

E. No-flap landing

1. *Description.* The applicant may be asked to perform a no-flap visual approach to a point where, in the judgment of the examiner, a landing to a full stop on the appropriate runway could be safely made.

2. *Acceptable performance guidelines.* Traffic pattern airspeeds shall be controlled within plus or minus 5 knots of that recommended for the type airplane being used and the appropriate airplane configuration until reaching final approach. Airspeed on the final approach shall be controlled within −0 to +10 knots of reference speed with appropriate wind/gust factor adjustment as recommended by the operating instructions for the airplane being used. Threshold airspeeds, also, shall be as recommended by those instructions with appropriate wind/gust factor adjustments.

F. Rejected landing

1. *Description.* The applicant may be asked to demonstrate one rejected landing from a point approximately 100 feet above the runway threshold. This maneuver may be combined with simulated instrument approaches but instrument conditions need not be simulated below 200 feet above the runway.

2. *Acceptable performance guidelines.* Airspeed on the final approach shall be controlled within −0 to +10 knots of reference speed with appropriate wind/gust factor adjustments as recommended by the operating instructions for the airplane being used. Threshold speeds, also, shall be recommended by those instructions with appropriate wind/gust factor adjustments. During the transition to a climb, the applicant shall maintain positive airplane control and appropriate airspeeds, operate the flaps and gear in proper sequence, and use correct power and trim settings.

G. Collision avoidance precautions

1. *Description.* The applicant is expected to exercise conscientious and continuous surveillance of the airspace in which the airplane is being operated to guard against potential mid-air collision. In addition to "see and avoid" practices, he is expected to use VFR Advisory Service at nonradar facilities, Airport Advisory Service at non-tower airports or FSS locations, and Radar Traffic Information Service, where available.

2. *Acceptable performance guidelines.* The applicant shall maintain continuous vigilance for other aircraft and take immediate actions necessary to avoid any situation which could result in a mid-air collision. Extra precautions shall be

taken, particularly in areas of congested traffic, to ensure that his view of other aircraft is not obstructed by his aircraft's structure. When traffic advisory service is used, the applicant shall understand terminology used by the radar controller in reporting positions of other aircraft. Failure to maintain proper surveillance shall be disqualifying.

H. Wake turbulence avoidance

1. Description. The applicant may be asked to explain wing-tip vortices, their characteristics and associated hazards. He should follow the recommended courses of action to remain clear of wake turbulence.

2. Acceptable performance guidelines. The applicant shall identify the conditions and locations in which wake turbulence may be encountered and adjust his flight path in a manner to avoid these areas. Failure to follow recommended courses of action for minimizing the possibility of flying into wingtip vortices shall be disqualifying.

VI. NORMAL AND ABNORMAL PROCEDURES

Objective. To determine that the applicant has a practical knowledge of the systems and devices appropriate to the airplane type.

A. Systems and devices

1. Description. The applicant may be asked to demonstrate his knowledge regarding the proper use of the systems and devices listed below which are appropriate to the type airplane, as the person conducting the check finds necessary to determine the required proficiency: (a) anti-icing and de-icing systems, (b) auto-pilot systems, (c) automatic or other approach aids, (d) stall warning, stall avoidance and stability augmentation devices, (e) airborne radar devices, (f) hydraulic and electrical system failures, (g) landing gear and flap system failures, (h) airborne Nav/Com equipment failures, (i) oxygen and environmental systems.

2. Acceptable performance guidelines. Performance shall be evaluated on the basis of the applicant's demonstration of knowledge of the procedures for the airplane used and the judgment displayed.

VII. EMERGENCY PROCEDURES

Objective. To determine that the applicant has an adequate knowledge of, and the ability to perform emergency procedures appropriate to the airplane being used.

A. Emergency procedures

1. Description. The applicant may be asked to demonstrate his knowledge regarding the proper emergency procedures outlined in the manufacturer's published recommendations for the type airplane used, as determined necessary by the examiner.

2. Acceptable performance guidelines. Performance shall be evaluated on the basis of the applicant's demonstration of knowledge of the emergency procedures referred to above for the airplane used, the judgment displayed, and the accuracy of his operations.

(End of material from FAA AC 61-57 on flight test requirements for the type rating.)

AIRCRAFT TYPE RATINGS ISSUED BY THE FAA

Airplanes

1 MANUFACTURERS	2 MODEL DESIGNATORS	3 PRIOR DESIGNATORS	4 DESIGNATORS AFTER 7/1/70
AERO COMMANDER, Division, North American Rockwell Corp. USA	1121 Jet Commander	Aero Commander 1121	AC-1121 CJ 1123
ARMSTRONG-WHITWORTH AIRCRAFT, LTD.,UK	Argosy AW 650	Armstrong-Whitworth AW-650	AW-650
BOEING CO., The USA	B-17 247-D 314 S-307, SA-307 377, C-97, YC-97 707, 720, C-135 727 737 747	Boeing B-17 Boeing 247 Boeing 314 Boeing 307 Boeing 377 Boeing 707/720 Boeing 727 Boeing 737	B-B17 B-247 B-314 B-307 B-377 B-707 B-720 B-727 B-737 B-747
BREGUET, France	Fauvette 905A		BG-905
BRISTOL AIRCRAFT, LTD., UK	Britannia 305		BR-305
BRITISH AIRCRAFT CORP., UK	BAC 1-11	BAC 1-11	BA-111
BUSHMASTER AIRCRAFT CORP., USA	Bushmaster 2000		BU-2000
CANADAIR, LTD. Canada	CL-44, OC-6 CL-215-1A10	Canadair C-44	CL-44
CHASE (Also Roberts Aircraft Co.), USA	YC-122	Chase YC-122	YC-122
CONSOLIDATED VULTEE AIRCRAFT	(See General Dynamics Corp.)		
CONVAIR	(See General Dynamics Corp.)		

CURTISS-WRIGHT CORP., USA	Commando CW20	Curtiss-Wright C-46	CW-46
DART AIRCRAFT CORP.	(See General Dynamics Corp.)		
DASSAULT, GENERAL AERONAUTIQUE MARCEL, DASSAULT, France	Mystere 20 Falcon, Fan Jet	GAMD/SUD-20	DA-20
de HAVILLAND AIRCRAFT OF CANADA, LTD., Canada (See Hawker Siddeley)	Caribou 4A, USAF C-7A, Army CV-2	de Havilland Caribou DH-4	DH-4
DEE HOWARD CO. USA	Howard 500	Howard 500	HW-500
DOUGLAS AIRCRAFT CO.	(See McDonnell Douglas)		
FAIRCHILD HILLER CORP., USA	Friendship F-27 F-227, C-119C	Fairchild F-27/227	FA-27 FA-227
FOKKER, Netherlands	Fellowship F-28		FK-28
FORD MOTOR CORP. USA	Tri-Motor 4-AT 5-AT	Ford 5	FO-5
GENERAL DYNAMICS CORP., USA	PB2Y-3, PB2Y-5	Consolidated-Vultee PB2Y	CV-PB2Y
	PB4Y-2, QP-4B	Consolidated-Vultee P4Y-2	CV-P4Y
	PBY-5, 28-4, 28-5	Consolidated-Vultee PBY-5	CV-PBY5
	LB-30, C-87A	Consolidated-Vultee LB-30	CV-LB30
	240, 340, 440, T-29 C-131	Convair 240/340/440	CV-240 CV-340 CV-440
	22, 22M (880)(990)	Convair 880/990	CV-880 CV-990
	Napier-Eland Mark I, Mark II Allison Propjet	Napier Eland Convair Mark I/II	CV-N1 CV-N2
	Convair 340/440	Allison Convair 340/440	CV-A340 CV-A440
	Dart Convair 240 340,440	Convair 600/640	CV-600 CV-640
GRUMMAN AIRCRAFT AND ENGINEERING CORP., USA	TBF, TBM	Grumman TBF	G-TBM
	G-73 Mallard G-64, SA-16	Grumman G-73	G-73

	Albatross	Grumman SA-16	G-SA16
	G-159 Gulfstream	Grumman G-159	G-159
	VC-4A, TC-4C		
	G-1159 Gulfstream	Grumman G-1159	G-1159
HANDLEY PAGE AIRCRAFT CO. LTD., UK	Herald 300	Handley Page 300	HP-300
HAMBURGER FLUGZEUBAU, G.M.B.H. West Germany	Hansa Jet 320		HF-320
HAWKER SIDDELEY AVIATION, LTD., UK	DH-125	Hawker Siddeley 125 HS-125	HS-125
	DH-106, Comet 4C	de Havilland 4C	HS-106
	DH-114 Heron	Hawker Siddeley 114	HS-114
HOWARD AERO CORP. (See Dee Howard Co.)			
ISRAELI AIRCRAFT, LTD., Israel (See Aero Commander)	Commodore Jet 1123		AC 1121 CJ 1123
LEAR JET INDUSTRIES GATES, CORP., USA	23 & 24 25	Lear 23/24 Lear 25	LR-23 LR-24 LR-25
LOCKHEED AIRCRAFT CORP. USA	Lightning P-38	Lockheed P-38	L-P38
	B-34, PV-1, PV-2	Lockheed B-34	L-B34
	Series 14	Lockheed 14	L-14
	18, C-57, C-60 R-50 & Learstar	Lockheed 18	L-18
	Constellation Series	Lockheed Constellation	L-49
	Electra 188, PV-3	Lockheed 188	L-188
	JetStar 1329, C-140	Lockheed 1329	L-1329
	T-33, TV-2	Lockheed T-33	L-T33
	382, C-130	Lockheed 382	L-382
	300, C-141	Lockheed 300	L-300
	L-1011 Tri-Star		L-1011
MARTIN-MARIETTA CORP., USA	B-26 Marrauder	Martin B-26C	M-B26
	PBM-5, C-162 Mariner	Martin PBM-5	M-PBM5
	202, 404	Martin 202/404	M-202 M-404
McDONNELL DOUGLAS AIRCRAFT CORP.	A-20	Douglas A-20	DC-A20
	A-24, SBD	Douglas A-24	DC-A24
	B-26	Douglas B-26	DC-B26
	B-18	Douglas B-18	DC-B18
	B-23, UC-67	Douglas B-23	DC-B23

	DC-2, C-32, C-34 C-39, C-42	Douglas DC-2	DC-2
	DC-3, C-47, C-117 (A thru C)	Douglas DC-3	DC-3
	Super DC-3, C-117D	Douglas DC-3S	DC-3S
	DC-4, C-54	Douglas DC-4	DC-4
	DC-6, DC-7, C118	Douglas DC6/DC7	DC-6 DC-7
	DC-8	Douglas DC-8	DC-8
	DC-9	Douglas DC-9	DC-9
	DC-10		DC-10
MORANE SAULNIER France	MS760	Morane-Saulnier MS760	MS-760
NIHON AEROPLANE MANUFACTURING CO. LTD., Japan	YS-11	NAMC YS-11	YS-11
NORD AVIATION France	262A Super Broussard	Nord 262A	ND-262
NORTH AMERICAN ROCKWELL CORP. USA	B-25 Mitchell	North American B-25	N-B25
	NA-265 Sabreliner T-39	North American NA-265	N-265
NORTHROP CORP. USA	P-61 Blackwidow	Northrop P-61	NH-P61
PIAGGIO Italy	Piaggio-Douglas 808	Piaggio Douglas PD808	P-808
SIKORSKY AIRCRAFT, DIVI- SION OF UNITED AIRCRAFT CORP., USA	VS-44A S-43 Series	Sikorsky VS-44 Sikorsky S-43	SK-44 SK-43
SUD-AVIATION, France	SE Caravelle I, III, VIR	SUD 210	S-210
VICKERS-ARMSTRONG BRITISH AIRCRAFT CORP., UK	700 & 800 Series	Vickers Viscount	VC-700 VC-800

Helicopters

1	2	3	4
MANUFACTURERS	MODEL DESIGNATORS	PRIOR DESIGNATORS	DESIGNATORS AFTER 7/1/70
BOEING VERTOL	107-II, H-46 Kawasaki KV107-II	Vertol 107-II	BV-107
VERTOL	H-21	Vertol 44	BV-44
SIKORSKY	S-58 Series, H-34 Series	Sikorsky S-58, S-58IT	SK-58
SIKORSKY	S-61 Series H-3 Series	Sikorsky S-61	SK-61
SIKORSKY	S-64 Series, CH-54A Series, HH-53A	Sikorsky S-64 Sikorsky S-65	SK-64 SK-65
SUD AVIATION	SA321F; SA330F		S-321 S-330

The following is a list of helicopters weighing 12,500 pounds or less on which type ratings are issued to holders of airline transport pilot certificates only:

BELL	47 Series, H-13 Series	Bell 47	BH-47
BELL	204-B, UHI-B, -D, H205A	Bell 204	BH-204
BELL	206A	Bell 206	BH-206
BELL	212	Bell 212	BH-212
BRANTLY	B-2 (YHO3BR)	Brantly B-2	BY-2
BRANTLY	305	Brantly 305	BY-305
ENSTROM	F-28	Enstrom F-28	EN-28
HILLER	UH-12 Series H-23 Series	Hiller UH-12	HH-12
FAIRCHILD	FH-1100	FH-1100	FA-1100
HUGHES	269 Series	Hughes 269A	HU-269
HUGHES	500, 369 Series	Hughes 500	HU-500

KAMAN	K-190A	Kaman K-190A	KM-190
	K-225	Kaman K-225	KM-225
	K-240, HTK-1	Kaman K-240	KM-240
	K-600		KM-600
LOCKHEED	Lockheed California 286	Lockheed California 285	L-286
OMEGA	12D1	Omega 12D1	OM-12
PIASECKI	HRP-1, HRP-2	Piasecki HRP	PI-HRP
SIKORSKY	R-4B	Sikorsky R-4B	SK-4
SIKORSKY	R-5A, YR-6A R-6A, HOS-1	Sikorsky R-5A	SK-5
SIKORSKY	S-51	Sikorsky S-51	SK-51
SIKORSKY	S-52 Series	Sikorsky S-52	SK-52
SIKORSKY	S-55, H-19 Series	Sikorsky S-55	SK-55
SIKORSKY	S-62A Series	Sikorsky S-62	SK-62
SILVERCRAFT	SPA-SH4		SI-4
SCHEUTZOW	Model B		SC
SUD AVIATION	SE 3130, SE 313B; SE 3160, SA 316B; SA 3180, SA 318B, SA 318C	Sud Alouette II/III	S-3130
SUD AVIATION	SO 1221	Sud Djinn	S-1221

8.

Aircraft performance charts

TYPES OF AIRCRAFT PERFORMANCE CHARTS

Tables are compact arrangements of conditions and performance values in orderly sequence, usually arranged in rows and columns. These charts require interpolation to determine intermediate values for particular flight conditions or performance.

Graphs are pictorial representations of the relationship between at least two variables. Aircraft performance graphs are usually the straight-line or curved-line types. The straight-line graph is a result of two values that vary at a constant rate (Figures 14 and 15), while a curved-line graph is a result of two values that vary at a changing rate (Figures 16 and 17). Like tables, graphs require interpolation to determine intermediate values.

INTERPOLATION OF AIRCRAFT PERFORMANCE CHARTS

To interpolate means to compute intermediate values between a series of given values. In other words, divide the distance or interval into as many units as necessary to include the desired value as one of the values. For example, find the value of X:

U	Z
12	22

U	V	W	X	Y	Z
12	14	16	18	20	22

X = 18

Performance tables. For a practical problem, determine the takeoff distance of a particular light twin from the table in Fig. 12. Assume at takeoff the pressure altitude is 3,000 feet, OAT is 65°F., and headwind is 10 mph. Underlined on the table are the given values for altitude and headwind. Circled are the values that need interpolation.

TAKEOFF DISTANCES - FEET
(over a 50-Foot Obstacle)

Use takeoff power on both engines (limiting manifold pressure, 3400 RPM) with mixture in auto-rich position, cowl flaps full open, flaps set at 1/4 (10°). Attain full engine power before releasing brakes. Climb out at 106 mph (92 knots) CAS. Limit power setting to 2 minutes.

TAKEOFF GROSS WEIGHT - 8,000 POUNDS

Pressure Altitude Feet	Wind Velocity MPH	°F OUTSIDE AIR TEMPERATURE				
		-25	0	25	50	75
	-10	2053	2282	2535	2808	3098
	0	1758	1955	2172	2406	2656
3000	+10	1481	1648	1832	2030	2242
	+20	1225	1364	1517	1684	1860
	+30	990	1104	1230	1365	1510

$$\frac{65° - 50°}{75° - 50°} = \frac{15}{25} \text{ or } \frac{3}{5}$$

65° is the point
3/5 of the interval
between 50° and 75°

3/5 X 212 = 127.2

2242
- 2030
212

2030 + 127.2 = 2157.2

2157.2 is the point
3/5 of the interval
between 2030 and
2242 feet

Fig. 12.

In the margin to the right of the graph, a position or relationship of 65° with the two given values was determined. This relationship was applied to the two takeoff distances given to find the takeoff value for a 65° temperature. Under existing conditions, takeoff distance is 2,157.2 feet. The same problem can be solved quickly on the computer by setting up a 15 to 25 ratio and observing the proportionate increased takeoff distance opposite 212 as shown. (Figure 13).

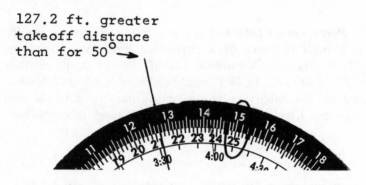

127.2 ft. greater takeoff distance than for 50°→

Fig. 13.

Performance graphs. Aircraft performance charts which utilize a graph are made up of two components: a basic grid of vertical and horizontal lines, each representing a value of a condition, and either straight or curved lines at an angle to the grid lines representing values of a third condition. By plotting an intersection of known values of two conditions, the value of the unknown condition can be determined at the same intersection.

Find the density altitude with these existing conditions: Airport elevation 7,795 feet, OAT 25°F., and altimeter setting 29.70. (Fig. 14).

Solution. The chart requires pressure altitude, which is determined from the conversion table at the right of the graph. 7,795 + 205 = 8,000 feet pressure altitude.

Step 1: Draw a line parallel to the vertical lines from the 25°F point (A) to the diagonal 8,000 feet pressure altitude line.

Step 2: Draw line B representing a value of 8,000 feet parallel to the horizontal density altitude lines so that it intersects the density altitude scale on the left margin of the graph.

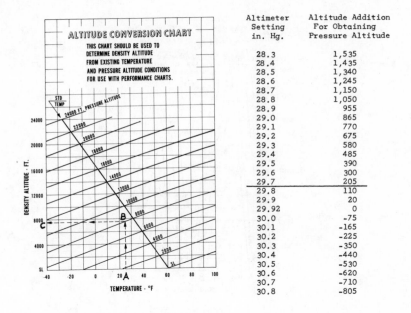

Altimeter Setting in. Hg.	Altitude Addition For Obtaining Pressure Altitude
28.3	1,535
28.4	1,435
28.5	1,340
28.6	1,245
28.7	1,150
28.8	1,050
28.9	955
29.0	865
29.1	770
29.2	675
29.3	580
29.4	485
29.5	390
29.6	300
29.7	205
29.8	110
29.9	20
29.92	0
30.0	-75
30.1	-165
30.2	-225
30.3	-350
30.4	-440
30.5	-530
30.6	-620
30.7	-710
30.8	-805

Fig. 14.

Step 3: The intersection of line B with the density altitude scale lies on about the 7,500 foot value (C). The density altitude is approximately 7,500 feet.

Combined graphs. Some aircraft performance charts incorporate two or more graphs into one when an aircraft flight performance involves several conditions. A simple combination of graphs is illustrated in Fig. 15. Choose the conditions that are appropriate and solve on that portion of the graph. Sample problems for several conditions are solved under the graph.

Another combined graph is illustrated in Fig. 16. It requires three functions to solve for takeoff distance with adjustments for air density, gross weight, and headwind conditions. The first function converts pressure altitude to density altitude. The right margin of this portion of the graph, even though it is not numbered, represents density altitude and starts the second function, the effect of gross weight on takeoff distance. The right margin of

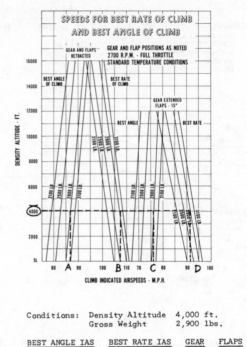

Conditions: Density Altitude   4,000 ft.
              Gross Weight   2,900 lbs.

BEST ANGLE IAS	BEST RATE IAS	GEAR	FLAPS
A - 87 mph	B - 107 mph	up	0°
C - 77 mph	D - 92 mph	down	15°

Fig. 15.

this section represents takeoff distance with no wind and
starts the final phase of correcting for effect of headwind.
A sample problem is illustrated below the graph. A more
complex graph combines many functions intermingled on
one basic grid to avoid using several graphs. However
complicated a graph may appear, the procedure for solution
is the same as for the simple graph. In Fig. 17 one grid is
used with a choice of three different altitude scales. It also
accomodates two conditions for oxygen consumption. To
solve, construct an intersection using the appropriate
altitude scale and the curved line representing the oxygen
cylinder pressure for the condition of intended use. Trans-
fer the intersection value to the bottom scale via the vertical
lines. Read the duration of the oxygen for one man and

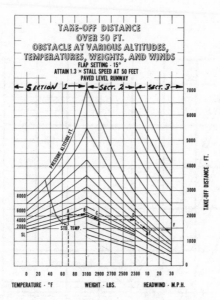

A - Conversion to Density Altitude.
B - Carry results to 2nd section of graph.
C - Parallel lines to gross wt. for loading.
D - Carry results to 3rd section of graph.
E - Parallel lines to headwind component.
F - Carry results to edge of graph for
    takeoff distance readout.

Fig. 16.

divide the results by the number of users for the total
duration of oxygen. Plotted on the graph are six values
of oxygen duration at an altitude of 25,000 feet and initial
oxygen pressure of 1,100 psi. The variable conditions are
cabin pressure and flow of oxygen (normal or 100%).
Result "A" (360 minutes) is the duration resulting from
1.0 psi. pressurization and 100% oxygen flow. "F" is the
duration of oxygen if normal flow is used.

Helpful hints. Before any attempt is made to interpret
a performance chart, carefully check the scales. Information
you use is sometimes given in knots and the chart may be
calibrated in mph. The same warning is appropriate for
Centigrade and Fahrenheit. Check the chart for footnotes
which might affect the solution you get. Sometimes it is

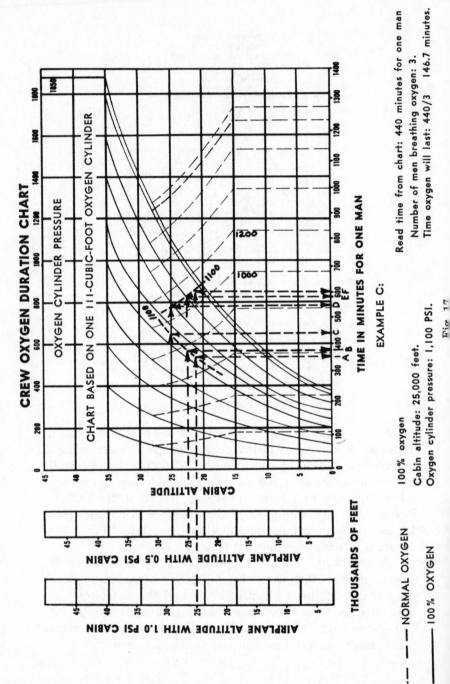

CREW OXYGEN DURATION CHART

OXYGEN CYLINDER PRESSURE

CHART BASED ON ONE 111-CUBIC-FOOT OXYGEN CYLINDER

TIME IN MINUTES FOR ONE MAN

EXAMPLE C:

100% oxygen
Cabin altitude: 25,000 feet.
Oxygen cylinder pressure: 1,100 PSI.

Read time from chart: 440 minutes for one man
Number of men breathing oxygen: 3.
Time oxygen will last: 440/3   146.7 minutes.

THOUSANDS OF FEET

AIRPLANE ALTITUDE WITH 0.5 PSI CABIN

AIRPLANE ALTITUDE WITH 1.0 PSI CABIN

CABIN ALTITUDE

— — NORMAL OXYGEN

——— 100% OXYGEN

Fig. 17

not necessary to interpolate as closely as was done in this Exam-O-Gram, but you should round off figures to be on the safe side.

Value of performance charts. Aircraft performance charts are of great value to determine performance for specific circumstances. Don't overlook the potential of these same charts to reveal and enrich the knowledge of operating characteristics of the aircraft. By plotting as many conditions as you have encountered, or anticipate encountering, you will develop a better overall mental image of the operating characteristics and limits of your aircraft and equipment.

Graphs are somewhat like pictures in that a person can retain more knowledge through use of the sense of sight. It is much easier to remember trends of performance or aerodynamics principles through a mental image of a line on a graph than through the printed or spoken word. Like pictures, good performance charts are worth a thousand words.

(IFR Pilot Exam-O-Gram No. 32, FAA)

9.

Tips for the multiengine instructor

1. It sounds elementary, but don't attempt to instruct in a light twin unless you are current and qualified in that model. True, they're all airplanes, but they're all different. For example, on a Cessna 310F, if both an engine-driven fuel pump and an auxiliary fuel pump fail on the same side, fuel can be supplied to the failing engine by cross-feeding from the opposite main tank with the use of the operative auxiliary fuel pump in that tank. However, on a Cessna 310G the fuel system is slightly different, and the failing engine cannot be supplied with fuel from the opposite tank as on the 310F. As another example, on a D-50 Twin Bonanza, fuel may be cross-fed from the main tanks only, while on the E-50 Twin Bonanza, fuel is cross-fed from the auxiliary tanks only. In still another instance, both the Beech Baron series and the Cessna 310 series employ a handcrank for emergency gear-down extension of the electrically operated gear, but the gear switch must be positioned to *neutral* on the Cessna 310's and to *down* on the Barons for manual extension.

2. If your light twin has no brakes on the instructor's side, be sure your student fully understands the use of toe brakes. Some students arrive at the multiengine stage having flown aircraft equipped with handbrakes only.

3. Be prepared for the student to demonstrate "Murphy's Law". For example, he may pull back prop controls instead of throttles, mixtures instead of props, etc. He may even reach for the gear handle or switch instead of the flaps. Instruct him to leave flaps down throughout the landing roll, raising them only after turning off the runway. On touch-and-go landings, instruct your student that you will be responsible for raising the flaps.

4. In conducting single-engine practice, be prepared for the student to feather the wrong engine, turn the fuel off to the good engine, or turn the magnetos off on the good engine. If the student inadvertently shuts down the fuel, mags, or mixture on the good engine, retard the throttle before restoring power, otherwise the sudden surge of power may be damaging to the engine.

5. Be prepared for the student to apply the wrong rudder pressure when you cut an engine This would be particularly hazardous during or shortly after takeoff, so be ready to counteract such action with your own rudder pressure. Also be ready to restore power as a further means of preventing a dangerous yaw.

6. If you are flying two or more light-twin types, remember that gear and flap controls may be exactly reversed between models, as may throttle, prop, or mixture controls. Look before you touch.

7. When practicing feathering, make sure you are at least 3,000 feet above the ground and in close proximity to a good airport.

8. Before feathering an engine, make sure the generator is functioning on the remaining engine. Then if you encounter difficulty in re-starting you'll have a generator to keep your battery up. Otherwise you might find it embarrassing to have feathered the engine with the only good generator, thereby necessitating an actual single-engine landing.

9. If you are unable to re-start an engine with normal procedures, put the aircraft in a shallow dive while engaging the starter; extra speed may help in windmilling the engine out of feather. If you have observed tip No. 7 you'll be able to sacrifice some altitude in this experiment without your position becoming critical.

10. Engine re-starts after feathering offer another opportunity for "Murphy's Law". Be prepared for the student to shut down the good engine while attempting to re-start the feathered engine.

11. The multiengine instructor can find a good deal of useful information in the following reprint of *Survival Tips for Light-Twin Multiengine Flight Instructors* prepared by the FAA's General Aviation District Office at Van Nuys, Calif.

ENGINE FAILURE ON TAKEOFF

Objective. Provide the trainee with the skill and knowledge required to cope with an engine failure during any flight phase from start of takeoff roll to reaching a maneuvering altitude.

Description. All simulated engine failures for this maneuver will be produced by retarding a throttle. There are two speeds which are of vital importance in any actual or simulated engine failure during takeoff: V_{mc} and V_{yse}.

The trainee will state these two speeds aloud as he pulls onto the runway to begin takeoff. There are three situations through which each takeoff must pass before reaching a safe altitude for maneuvering:

1. On takeoff roll before becoming airborne when engine fails.

2. Airborne at a speed below V_{yse} when engine fails.

3. Airborne at a speed at or above V_{yse} when engine fails.

In situation 1 the operating engine will be throttled and the takeoff aborted. (*Note*: There is no certification requirement that a light twin have any climb performance at V_{mc}.)

Situation 2 usually will require an immediate landing because of altitude loss required to increase speed to V_{yse}. The trainee must consider variables such as remaining runway, weight, altitude, and single-engine performance in deciding whether it is safer to land or accelerate to V_{yse} and continue flight. (*Note*: The minimum speed for all *normal* takeoffs is $V_{mc}+5$. This assures having air control before losing ground control.

Situation 3 leaves but one major decision to the pilot: where to land with maximum safety consistent with the performance limitations of his aircraft. After reaching V_{yse} and before reaching a safe maneuvering altitude, he must decide whether to land on the remaining runway, land in the best possible airport area, or, performance permitting, continue climbing on one engine to a safe maneuvering altitude and return to the airport for landing. (*Caution*: The instructor must closely follow the trainee's actions to insure correct responses. Inadvertent movement of any control in the wrong manner can jeopardize safety.

Standards. Situation 1: immediately reduce power on the operating engine and bring the aircraft safely to a full stop on the runway.

Situation 2: maintain a straight flight path and make a safe engine-out landing. Continue flight *only* when it is less hazardous to do so.

Situation 3: maintain a straight flight path, correctly identify and simulate feathering of the failed engine, maintain $V_{yse}+5$ mph.

ENGINE-OUT MINIMUM CONTROL SPEED DEMONSTRATION

Objective. Provide the trainee with an understanding of V_{mc}, and its effects on aircraft operation.

Description. V_{mc} is the minimum speed at which an airplane is controllable with one engine windmilling and the other at takeoff power with the aircraft in the most adverse configuration. For V_{mc} demonstrations the aircraft will be flown as nearly as possible under the following conditions: at highest altitude where takeoff power can be developed, but at no time below 1,500 feet above the ground; landing gear retracted; flaps at takeoff setting; center of gravity at the aft limit; critical engine windmilling; and takeoff power on the operating engine. (*Note*: since V_{mc} is a function of power it will be possible on any light twin to attempt this demonstration at an altitude where the aircraft will reach stall speed prior to V_{mc}.)

The V_{mc} demonstration is entered with the aircraft configured as above at an airspeed between best angle of climb speed (single engine) and best rate of climb speed (single engine). Airspeed is reduced at the rate of one mph per second. Rudder may be used as required to full deflection but aileron is limited to that which produces a maximum of 5° wing down into the operating engine. When a constant heading can no longer be maintained, *note the airspeed.* Effect a recovery to normal flight by lowering the nose and advancing power on the windmilling engine. (*Note*: rapid rolling tendencies may develop if the airspeed reduction is too abrupt or if attitude is such that the aircraft stalls before reaching V_{mc}. In this event, immediate reduction of power on the operating engine may be required to effect a prompt recovery.)

Standards. The maneuver should be entered without abrupt changes in attitude, altitude, or airspeed.

Airspeed should be reduced one mph per second.

Full rudder may be applied, but not more than 5° bank into the operating engine at V_{mc}.

Positive and coordinated recovery should be made to normal flight without excessive bank or pitch changes.

STALLS AND APPROACHES TO STALLS

Objective. Teach the trainee to recognize an approaching stall and execute a proper recovery from both approach to stalls and full stalls.

Description. Conditions of flight for stalls and approach to stalls:

1. Stalls must be accomplished at a safe altitude but not less than 3,000 feet above the terrain.

2. Both power-on and power-off stalls in landing and cruise configurations are required. Power requirements for power-on stalls must be 65% of maximum continuous power.

3. Stalls must be executed in straight and turning flight using approximately 30° of bank.

Stall and recovery—With trim control adjusted for straight flight at 1.5 V_{s1}, the speed must be reduced by means of the elevator control until the speed is slightly above the stalling speed, then the elevator control must be pulled back at a rate such that the airplane speed reduction does not exceed 1 mph per second until a stall is produced, or until the control reaches the stop.

Recovery should be initiated when the nose pitches through level flight attitude or when the elevator hits the stop on aircraft with limited nose-up elevator control. Stall recoveries should be accomplished with coordinated flight control usage, the smooth application of power, when applicable, and the least loss of altitude consistent with the prompt recovery of control effectiveness. Power-off stall recoveries should also be accomplished. (*Note*: deactivation of stall warning devices is prohibited in airplanes for which they are required equipment.)

Approach to stalls and recovery—Entries to approach to stalls must be accomplished in the same manner as entries to stalls. Recoveries must be initiated at the first indication of an approaching stall by relaxing back-pressure and smoothly returning to straight and level flight by the coordinated use of all flight and power controls.

Standards. The trainee must perform the above maneuvers with smooth coordinated control pressures and positive airplane control with the least loss of altitude consistent with the prompt recovery of control effectiveness.

PROPELLER FEATHERING AND UNFEATHERING

Objective. To develop in the trainee the proper procedures and proficiency for feathering and unfeathering an inoperative engine.

Description.

Feathering—at a safe altitude (minimum 3,000 feet above the terrain) and within landing distance of an adequate airport, an engine will be cut with mixture or fuel selector. The following procedures are to be followed then:

1. Mixture and power as required.
2. Gear and flaps as required.
3. Determine which engine failed and prove it by closing the throttle on the dead engine.
4. If unable to remedy cause of failure, feather.
5. Turn towards airport and contact tower.
6. Clean up dead engine in accordance with manufacturer's instructions.
7. Monitor engine instruments on operating engine and adjust power, cowl flaps, and speed as necessary.
8. Maintain altitude with airspeed at least V_{yse} or above if possible.

Unfeathering—Unfeathering must be accomplished in accordance with the manufacturer's recommendations.

Standards. Proficiency will be evaluated on the basis of maintaining desired heading, airspeed and altitude;

prompt identification of the failed engine; and the accuracy of shutdown and restart procedures.

MANEUVERING WITH AN INOPERATIVE ENGINE

Objective. To develop proficiency in the precise control of the airplane with simulated engine failure.

Description. With one engine feathered or set at zero thrust power, the trainee must make turns into and away from the inoperative engine using banks up to 30°. Power must be used as required to maintain altitude and/or airspeed.

Standards. Trainee should maintain altitude within 100 feet of entry altitude (if the airplane has the capability) or the airspeed within 5 mph of V_{yse}.

SIMULATED ENGINE-OUT APPROACHES AND LANDINGS

Objective. To develop or maintain an acceptable level of performance in coping with simulated engine-out approaches and landings.

Description.

Conditions of flight.—All engine cuts must be in accordance with manufacturer's recommendations. All engine cuts must be accomplished with throttle when less than 1,000 feet above the terrain. Feathering must be simulated with zero thrust when less than 3,000 feet above the terrain.

The maneuver. Due to variations in performance, limitations, etc., of the many light twins, no specific flight path or procedure can be proposed that would be adequate in all single-engine emergencies. In most light twins, a single-engine approach and landing can be accomplished with the flight path and procedures almost identical to a normal approach and landing, with two noteworthy exceptions:

1. Speed on final should not get below V_{yse} until the landing is assured.

2. Full flaps should not be lowered until the landing is assured.

Standards. The trainee will obtain an acceptable level of performance and will accomplish a logical sequence of procedures compatible with the limitations of the airplane in its simulated emergency condition.

North American Rockwell Series-60 Sabreliner.

10.

Takeoff planning for light twins

This chapter is taken from a manual issued by the FAA mainly for the guidance of its own flight inspectors, but the material is of equal and practical value to Multiengine flight instructors and students in the field.

Takeoff planning is not a highly complicated procedure. One should think rather in terms of just using a little common sense. It is the same type of thinking that an old-timer would use flying single-engine airplanes. For instance, a pilot on a cross-country discovers that the pencil line on his map proceeds right down the middle of a swamp for 15 miles. The smart pilot wouldn't fly across the swamp just because the line on the map was there; he would skirt the edge and cross the swamp at a narrow point. Actually the pilot should have planned on going around the swamp long before he got there. The same is true if an emergency occurs on takeoff. The pilot should have already planned for that emergency if and when it does occur. In other words, be on the proper takeoff flight path.

V SPEEDS

Before the subject of takeoff technique in light multi-engine airplanes can be thoroughly discussed, several terms need to be defined. Following are the more important ones.

V_x: *the speed for best angle of climb.* At this speed the airplane will gain the greatest height for a given distance of forward travel. The speed is used for obstruction clearance with all engines operating. However, this speed will change when one engine is inoperative, and the speed for best angle of climb with one engine inoperative is designated as V_x (SE) (engine out).

V_y: *the speed for the best rate of climb.* This speed will give the maximum altitude for a given period of time with all engines operating. However, this speed will change when one engine is inoperative. The speed for the best rate of climb with one engine inoperative is designated V_y (SE) for twins.

V_{mc}: *the minimum control speed with the critical engine inoperative.* The term V_{mc} can be defined as "the minimum airspeed at which the airplane is controllable when the critical engine is suddenly made inoperative, with the remaining engine(s) producing takeoff power."

The Federal Aviation Regulations say that at V_{mc} the pilot must be able to do two things: (1) stop the turn which results when the critical engine is suddenly made inoperative, within 20° of the original heading, and (2) after recovery he must be able to maintain the airplane in straight flight with not more than 5° bank (wing down into good engine). This does not mean that the airplane will climb or even hold altitude. It means only that a heading can be maintained. These three speeds will be used further during the following discussion.

TAKEOFF FLIGHT PATH

A takeoff and climb flight path should be made so that all obstructions will be cleared. Anything between the point of takeoff and the point of landing which would interfere with that landing, assuming one engine out, is an obstruction and should play its part in one's planning.

Since an infinite number of takeoff and climb-out procedures are available, how is a pilot going to decide which one to use? The extremes in takeoff technique are (1) to hold the aircraft down and go over the far end of the runway at cruising speed only 30 feet high, or (2) to pull it off below V_{mc} (minimum control speed). If one considers the possibility of an engine failure somewhere during the takeoff, neither of these procedures makes much sense for the following reasons: drag increases as the square of the speed, so, for any increase in speed over and above the best engine-out climb speed, V_y (SE), the greater the drag, the less climb performance an airplane will have. At 123 mph the drag is approximately $1\frac{1}{2}$ times greater than it is at 100 mph. At 141 mph the drag has doubled, and at 200 mph the drag is approximately four times as great as at 100 mph. While the drag is increasing as the square of the velocity (V^2), the power required to maintain a velocity increases as the cube of that velocity (V^3).

A pilot who uses excessive speed on takeoff can suddenly discover he has converted all the energy produced by those engines into speed. There is the argument that a pilot can convert the excess speed to altitude, but this argument is not valid. As has been pointed out, power is being wasted to accelerate the airplane. Also, experience has shown that an unexpected engine failure surprises the pilot so that he will act as though he is "swimming in glue." By the time the shock wears off and he has control of the situation, the excess speed has deserted him and he is still only 30 feet from the ground. From this altitude he will still have to climb, with an engine out, to whatever height is needed to clear the obstructions at this particular field and get back to the end of the runway.

It has been shown that excess speed cannot be readily or completely coverted to altitude or distance to help you around the field; however, a plane will fly level much easier than it will climb. If the energy of all the engines (while they are operating) is initially converted to enough height above the field to permit the pilot to clear all the obstructions in level flight (maneuvering altitude) the problem is much simpler when an engine fails. If some extra height is available it can be traded for velocity or gliding distance.

On the other hand, trying to gain height too fast on takeoff can also be very dangerous because of control problems. If the airplane is in the air below V_{mc} when an engine fails, the pilot *might* avoid a crash by rapidly retarding the throttles, although the odds are not in favor of the pilot.

If a low and fast or slow and steep takeoff is not safe, then what technique should a pilot use?

It is obvious that the proper flight path must lie someplace between the too steep and too flat takeoff. To decide on the proper flight path the pilot must consider the capability of his airplane to climb with one engine inoperative. There is nothing in the FAR governing the certification of light multiengine airplanes which says they must fly (maintain altitude) while in the takeoff configuration and with an engine inoperative. In fact many of the light twins are not required to do this with one engine inoperative in any configuration, even at sea level. This is of major significance in the operations of FAR multiengine aircraft (i.e., light twins). With regard to performance (but not controllability) in the takeoff or landing configuration, the light multiengine aircraft is, in concept, merely a single engine aircraft with its power divided into two or more individual packages.

ATTAINING Vy SPEED

Another problem to consider is the technique of getting from a stand-still to V_y speed. The pilot should keep one hand on the yoke (if there is no hand-controlled nose steering) and the other hand on the throttles throughout the takeoff roll. The airplane should be on the ground until a speed is reached so that a smooth transition into the proper climb speed can be made. *Never leave the ground before V_{mc} is reached, and preferably $V_{mc} + 5$ mph.*

If an engine fails before leaving the ground, *stop*. If an engine fails *after* leaving the ground, the pilot must decide whether (1) to maintain V_y (single engine) while cleaning up the airplane and trying to continue, or (2) to close both throttles and land. However, waiting until the engine fails is not the time to make the decision! The decision should be made before the pilot taxis onto the runway. He should have considered the temperature, altitude of the airport, the weight of his airplane, and the length of the runway. Then he should have looked up the engine-out performance that his airplane would have under these conditions. That is when he should have made his decision on what course to follow if an engine should fail.

If the pilot decides to continue after an engine fails, he should:

1. Maintain V_y (single engine).
2. Check that RPM and MP are at takeoff power.
3. Maintain V_y (single engine).
4. Check that the flaps and gear have been retracted.
5. Maintain V_y (single engine).
6. Decide which engine is inoperative.
7. Maintain V_y (single engine).
8. Prove the inoperative engine by closing the throttle (completely) on the engine believed to be inoperative. If there is no change in rudder forces, then that is the inoperative engine.
9. Maintain V_y (single engine).
10. Feather prop on engine that has throttle closed.

11. Maintain V_y (single engine) even if settling into ground for it is better to land at V_y (single engine) speed than to spin in at some slower speed.

12. Check for fire; complete single-engine cleanup checklist as time permits while maneuvering to land.

In summary, the pilot should know, before he takes off, what the performance of his airplane is for temperature, altitude and weight of the airplane. He should be mentally prepared for an engine failure. If an engine does fail he should know what to do and how to do it. This proficiency can only be obtained and maintained by practicing engine failures with a competent instructor, simulating the engine failure during the takeoff, climbout, or in cruise.

A good flight path is one which leaves the ground above V_{mc} and climbs with all engines operating not slower than V_y (single engine) and not faster than V_y (both engines). The climb should be made to at least maneuvering altitudes with takeoff power on both engines; then power can be reduced to M.C. (maximum continuous) and the climb continued to traffic pattern altitude: the speed can then be increased to enroute climb speed and power reduced to climb power.

11.

Questions and answers for the oral test

No written examination is required for the FAA Multi-engine Rating. Before taking the actual flight test, however, each applicant is questioned orally on (1) the operation and performance of the particular aircraft in which the flight test will take place, and (2) multiengine procedures in general. To answer correctly the questions on (1) you are expected to be totally familiar with the airplane's flight manual, as emphasized throughout this guide. Unless the FAA examiner who asks the questions is satisfied that you know both the airplane and its manual, he isn't likely to authorize the actual flight test. As for the questions on *general* procedures, this chapter provides some fair samples. They are representative of the questions which the examiner may ask regardless of the aircraft model or type on which you are being examined.

   1. Q. *What is the critical engine?*
       A. It is that engine the failure of which has the the most adverse effect upon the airplane flight characteristics. On twin-engine aircraft which have clockwise rotat-

ing propellers (as viewed from the cockpit), the left engine is the critical one. With the left engine out, both the unbalanced thrust and torque of operating the right engine are pulling the aircraft to the left. (*Note:* British-made aircraft have engines which rotate in the opposite direction, and their torque effect is a yaw toward the right.) Many applicants for the Multiengine Rating erroneously answer this question by saying that the left engine is the critical one because it has the hydraulic pump or the generator or some such.

2. *Q. Is it permissible to turn toward the dead engine?*

A. Yes. The FAA *Multiengine Flight Test Guide* specifies that turns shall be made both toward and away from the dead engine. It is a common misconception that turns should not be made toward the dead engine, but in practice there is no reason why turns cannot be made either way. It will be noticed that recovery from turns into the dead engine will be slightly slower than normal due to the absence of the propeller airflow over the wing, but this does not prevent the turns being made.

3. *Q. Can the dead engine be identified by looking at the instruments?*

A. Usually not. The manifold pressure will be at the atmospheric pressure, which may not be very different from the cruising manifold pressure of the other engine. The propeller governor will keep the engine rpm very close to the rpm of the operating engine. The best method of identifying the dead engine is by the rudder pressure necessary to maintain straight flight. The "dead" foot is on the same side as the dead engine.

4. *Q. What should be one of the pilot's main considerations in making a single-engine landing?*

A. The pilot should realize that it is vitally important not to undershoot. In most light twins, it is possible to make a fairly steep approach with full flaps and power reduced on the good engine after the pilot has made sure of reaching the airport, and has approached slightly high.

5. *Q.* *In re-starting a feathered engine, what should be done about the radios, if anything?*

A. The radios should be turned off. The surge of current from starting the engines can be very damaging to transistor radios. These radios should be turned off on the initial ground starts for this reason, and the same applies to the air starts when the starter is used for unfeathering.

6. *Q.* *What are the most important speeds for the pilot to know in the event of an engine failure?*

A. The VMC, or minimum control speed; the single-engine best angle of climb speed; the single-engine best rate of climb speed. A pilot should not fly a light twin until he knows the VMC and SE Best Rate of Climb Speed for that model. All pilot handbooks show these two important speeds. In addition, some manuals give the SE best angle of climb speed.

7. *Q.* *Give an example of the use of the cross-feed.*

A. One purpose of most cross-feeds is to supply fuel to the operating engine (assuming one engine feathered) from the tanks in the opposite wing. The operating manual should be checked for the proper method of operation. For example, some aircraft specify that the electric fuel pump on the tank side be turned on, and on others it is the pump on the side of the operating engine.

8. *Q.* *Can a pilot who does not have a Multiengine Rating solo a twin-engine airplane?*

A. Yes. A Private or Commercial Pilot may solo a multiengine aircraft if a flight instructor, after giving him instruction in the twin, endorses in his log book that he is competent to solo that category and class of aircraft. Also, he may solo a multiengine aircraft if he has logged pilot-in-command time in it prior to November 1, 1973.

9. Q. *What is required of a rated multiengine pilot before he can carry passengers?*
     A. He must have 3 takeoffs and landings in the preceding 90 days in a multiengine airplane as sole manipulator of the controls. If the aircraft to be flown is a tailwheel airplane, the landings must have been made to a full stop in a multiengine tailwheel airplane, and it a type rating is required, in the same type.

10. Q. *Do the Federal Aviation Regulations require any specific number of hours of multiengine flying to qualify for the Multiengine Rating?*
     A. No. but an applicant for an additional class rating must present a logbook certified by a flight instructor that he has had dual instruction in this class of airplane and has been found competent in the appropriate pilot operations (see Chapt. 4).

11. Q. *May a pilot who does not hold a Multiengine Rating serve as safety pilot in a multiengine airplane operating under simulated instrument flight conditions?*
     A. No. FAR 91.21 requires that an appropriately rated pilot occupy the other control seat.

12. Q. *In performing the engine run-up on a tricycle-gear twin-engine airplane, should any precaution be taken concerning the nose-wheel?*
     A. Yes, the nose-wheel should be straight in order to prevent damage from a side-load on the wheel during engine run-up.

13. Q. *What does VMC mean to the pilot during takeoff in a light twin?*
     A. The airplane should be held on the ground until reaching VMC, the minimum control speed. Should an engine fail prior to this speed, the pilot should close

both throttles and bring the aircraft to a stop.

14. *Q. Is it permissible to have both hands on the control wheel during takeoff in a light twin-engine airplane?*

A. No, one hand must remain on the throttles. This allows the pilot to close the throttles instantly should an engine fail before VMC. It also serves the purpose of "guarding" the throttles to prevent any inadvertent creeping back.

15. *Q. Is it permissible to have both hands on the control wheel during landing in a light twin-engine airplane?*

A. No, one hand must remain on the throttles to give power without delay should it become necessary.

16. *Q. Is there a written examination for the Multiengine Rating?*

A. No, a flight test only.

17. *Q. Where is the allowable weight of the "useful load" shown?*

A. On the weight and balance report prepared by the manufacturer, or on superseding Form 337 if equipment was added or removed after the aircraft left the factory, or in the aircraft log book.

18. *Q. What does the "useful load" consist of?*

A. It is the weight of pilot and passengers, fuel, oil, and baggage.

19. *Q. What is the proper order of making power changes in a twin-engine aircraft with supercharged engines?*

A. To increase power, increase rpm first, then manifold pressure. To decrease power, decrease manifold pressure first, then rpm.

20. *Q. What effect does a high temperature have on the single-engine performance of a light twin-engine aircraft?*

A. The pilot should be aware that the single-engine climbing capacity of the airplane may be severely curtailed under these conditions. An airport at an elevation of 4,000 feet, with a temperature of 95° Fahrenheit, would have an actual *density* altitude of 7,200 feet. If the manufacturer showed the airplane as having a single-engine ceiling of 6,500 feet the airplane would be unable to climb, although an unwary pilot might think of 4,000 feet as being well below the single-engine ceiling.

21. *Q. Since some light twins use 80 octane fuel and others 100 octane, it may be of interest to the pilot to know the color of dye which is added to each fuel so that he might check for proper color in draining fuel sumps. What are these colors?*

A. A red dye is added to 80 octane and a green dye to 100 octane.

22. *Q. Some multiengine aircraft have three green lights to show that each wheel is down and locked. If one of these lights does not come on, what simple remedy can the pilot use to check whether the light or the gear is faulty?*

A. He can remove the bulb which does not light and replace it with one that did.

23. *Q. On some light twins the pilot can lower the gear and still find none of the gear lights burning. What is one probable reason?*

A. The navigation lights may be turned on. Many airplanes have the gear lights automatically dimmed when the nav lights come on, and the lights are too dim to be observed in daylight.

24. *Q. Why should "door locked" be included in the pre-takeoff checklist?*

A. Because the door which comes open in flight can set up a disturbance in the air flow, and the resultant buffeting impairs the airplane's flight characteristics.

25. Q. *In addition to the single-engine technique, what else should be remembered by the pilot making an emergency landing with an engine feathered?*

A. If the airport of his landing has a tower, airport advisory service, or even a unicom, he should make his situation known to the ground station for whatever assistance they can give in traffic priority or advisory to other aircraft operating in the area.

26. Q. *The applicant may be asked to define the "V" speeds, or to fill in the appropriate blanks on a form such as that shown in Fig. 18.*

27. Q. *What is the significance of the speed designated as 1.3 V_{so}?*

A. "For short field landings, the final approach from an altitude of at least 50 feet above the surface should be made at approximately 1.3 times the power-off stalling speed with gear and flaps extended. Descent should be controlled primarily with the throttles and the airspeed with the elevators. The round-out for landing should be accompanied by a smooth closing of the throttles, and result in little or no floating." (*FAA Multiengine Flight Test Guide.*)

28. Q. *What is the difference between indicated airspeed and calibrated airspeed?*

A. Indicated airspeed (*IAS*) is the speed read directly from the face of the airspeed indicator. Calibrated airspeed (*CAS*) is the indicated airspeed corrected for installation and instrument error.

29. Q. *What is true indicated airspeed (TIAS)?*

A. Calibrated airspeed and true indicated airspeed are the same. TIAS was formerly used, and this term appears in earlier airplane flight manuals and owner's manuals or flight handbooks.

AC Form 3140-26
Formerly AC Form 2474.

Aircraft Stall, Limitations and Performance Speeds

MAKE AND MODEL	V_x	V_y	V_{le}	V_{fe}	V_{so}	V_{sl}	V_a	$1.3V_{so}$	V_{no}	V_{ne}	Multi-Engine		
											V_{mc}	V_{xse}	V_{yse}
CESSNA 310	103	123	130	130	69	82	159	89.7	200	246	93	110	121

V_x - Best Angle of Climb Speed
V_y - Best Rate of Climb Speed
V_{le} - Maximum Landing Gear Extended Speed
V_{fe} - Maximum Flap Extended Speed
V_{so} - Power Off Stalling Speed Landing Configuration

V_{sl} - Stalling or Minimum Steady Flight Speed in a Specified Configuration
V_a - Design Maneuvering Speed
1.3 V_{so} - Fence Speed ($\frac{1}{4}$ Airspeed Correction)
V_{no} - Top of Green Arc
V_{ne} - Red Line

V_{mc} - Minimum Control Speed with the Critical Engine Inoperative
V_{xse} - Best Angle of Climb Speed, One Engine Inoperative
V_{yse} - Best Rate of Climb Speed, One Engine Inoperative

Fig. 18.

30. *Q. Where does the pilot find the "V" speeds shown in Fig. 18, and are they IAS or CAS (TIAS)?*

A. Calibrated airspeeds are used in airplane flight manuals, operating limitations, and placards. However, indicated airspeeds are given in the checklists and operating details of owner's manuals. (*Note*: Only aircraft weighing more than 6,000 pounds are required to have airplane flight manuals.)

31. *Q. In Fig. 18, which are IAS and which are CAS?*

A. V_x, V_y, V_{mc}, V_{xse} and V_{yse} are IAS. These are speeds the pilot needs to know at a glance from the airspeed indicator. All other speeds shown are CAS, except 1.3 V_{so}.

32. *Q. What about 1.3 V_{so}?*

A. The pilot must combine this figure by multiplying V_{so} times 1.3. Since V_{so} is CAS, the result would be CAS, and the pilot must refer to the airspeed correction table to convert to IAS. In the Cessna 310, however, there is no correction necessary at this speed (see Fig. 19).

AIRSPEED CORRECTION TABLE

Flaps 0°		Flaps 15°		Flaps 45°*	
IAS	TIAS	IAS	TIAS	IAS	TIAS
80	85	70	79	70	76
100	103	80	87	80	83
120	122	90	94	90	90
140	142	100	103	100	100
160	160	110	112	110	110
180	179	120	121	120	120
200	200	130	131	130	131
220	219	140	140	142	145
		150	150		
		160	159		

*Maximum flap speed 140 MPH

Fig. 19.

33. *Q. What is meant by "METO Power"?*

A. "METO" means Maximum Except Takeoff, and this is the highest power setting authorized for maximum continuous operation.

34.   *Q.   What is the significance of the two numbers used in the 80/87 or 100/130 designation of gasoline octanes?*

A.   Octane rating is the anti-knock quality of a gasoline—80 is the minimum anti-knock value in *lean* mixture, and 87 is the minimum anti-knock value in *rich* mixture. The same is true for 100/130.

35.   *Q.   Many light twins are fitted with a pressure carburetor. Why is this type of carburetor highly resistant to carburetor icing?*

A.   The fuel is injected under pressure into the airstream well beyond the venturi, and since ice usually forms in the venturi because of additional cooling caused by fuel vaporization in the venturi, this cause is eliminated.

Appendix

PART 1. DEFINITIONS AND ABBREVIATIONS

Category—as used with respect to the certification, ratings, privileges, and limitations of airmen, means a broad classification of aircraft, Examples include: airplane; rotorcraft; glider; and lighter-than-air.

Class—As used with respect to certification, ratings, privileges, and limitations of airmen, means a classification of aircraft within a category having similar operating characteristics. Examples include: single engine; multiengine; land; water; gyroplane; helicopter; airship; and free balloon.

Type—as used with respect to certification, ratings, privileges, and limitations of airmen, means a specific make and basic model of aircraft, including modifications thereto that do not change its handling or flight characteristics. Examples include: DC-7 and DC-7C; 1049G and 1049H; F-27 and F-27F.

PART 61. CERTIFICATION:
PILOTS AND FLIGHT INSTRUCTORS

61.5 *Certificates and ratings issued under this part.*

(b) The following ratings are placed on pilot certificates (other than student pilot) where applicable;

(1) Aircraft category ratings:
(i) Airplane.
(ii) Rotorcraft.
(iii) Glider.
(iv) Lighter-than air.
(2) Airplane class ratings:
(i) Single-engine land.
(ii) Multiengine land.
(iii) Single-engine sea.
(iv) Multiengine sea.
(3) Rotorcraft class ratings:
(i) Helicopter.
(ii) Gyroplane.
(5) Aircraft type ratings are listed in Advisory Circular 61-1, "Aircraft Type Ratings" (see also Chapt. 7 of this manual). This list includes ratings for the following:
(i) Large aircraft, other than lighter-than-air.
(ii) Small turbojet-powered airplanes.
(iii) Small helicopters for operations requiring an airline transport pilot certificate.
(iv) Other aircraft type ratings specified by the Administrator through aircraft type certificate procedures.

61.63 *Additional aircraft ratings (other than airline transport pilot).*

(c) *Class rating.* An applicant for an aircraft class rating to be added on his pilot certificate must—

(1) Present a logbook record certified by an authorized flight instructor showing that the applicant has received flight

instruction in the class of aircraft for which a rating is sought and has been found competent in the pilot operations appropriate to the pilot certificate to which his category rating applies; and

(2) Pass a flight test appropriate to his pilot certificate and applicable to the aircraft category and class rating sought.

(d) *Type rating.* An applicant for a type rating to be added on his pilot certificate must meet the following requirements:

(1) He must hold, or concurrently obtain, an instrument rating appropriate to the aircraft for which a type rating is sought.

(2) He must pass a flight test showing competence in pilot operations appropriate to the pilot certificate he holds and to the type rating sought.

(3) He must pass a flight test showing competence in pilot operations under instrument flight rules in an aircraft of the type for which the type rating is sought, or, in the case of a single pilot station airplane, meet the requirements of subdivision (i) or (ii) of this subparagraph, whichever is applicable.

(i) The applicant must have met the requirements of this subparagraph in a multiengine airplane for which the type rating is required.

(ii) If he does not meet the requirements of subdivision (i) of this subparagraph and he seeks a type rating for a single-engine airplane, he must meet the requirements of this subparagraph in either a single or multiengine airplane, and have the recent instrument experience set forth in 61.57(e) of this Part, when he applies for the flight test under subparagraph (2) of this paragraph.

(4) An applicant who does not meet the requirements of subparagraphs (1) and (3) of this paragraph may obtain a type rating limited to "VFR only." Upon meeting these instrument requirements or the requirements of 61.73 (e) (2), the "VFR only" limitation may be removed for the particular type of aircraft in which the competence is shown.

(5) When an instrument rating is issued to the holder of one or more type ratings, the type ratings on the amended certificate bear the limitation described in subparagraph (4) for each airplane type rating for which he has not shown his instrument competency under this paragraph.

Index

A free copy of our complete catalog
of airman training manuals and pilot-aids
will be sent to you promptly on request.
Just address a note or postcard to:

PAN AMERICAN NAVIGATION SERVICE
12021 VENTURA BLVD.
NORTH HOLLYWOOD, CALIF.